For Focal Sake!

D1634658

For Siân and Daniel...

*Hopefully this book will be out of print before
you're old enough to read!*

www.slang.ie

Many Tanks

Thanks to the following eejits for reviewing the various sections of the book…

James 'Nigsers' Mernin (Waterford)
Dominic 'Kuntyballix' Maguire (Antrim)
Ronan 'Owny Massif' Cleary (Dublin)
John 'Bucky' Kelly (Armagh)
Paul 'Sham' Savage (Galway)
Caroline 'Tome' Niland (Galway)
Mick 'Bogdized' Conlon (Mayo)
Declan 'Fear Glic' Ó Foghlú (Waterford)
Joy 'Half-pint' Redmond (Wexford)
Ann Marie 'Fine Day' O'Brien (Tipperary)
Donal 'The Rebel' McCarthy (Cork)
Raymond 'Titus' Foley (Cork / Waterford)
Brian 'Crusty Blaas' Delahunty (Kilkenny)
Ed 'Poulpeasty' Hendrick (Wexford)
Nicky 'Cra' McGrath (Kilkenny)
Sinead 'No Commint' Flynn (Leitrim)
Orla 'Tackie' Kelly (Limerick)
Christian 'Good' Ryder (Wicklow)
Susan 'BIFFO' Weldon (Offaly)
Paul 'Giant Dwarf' O'Reilly (Kildare)
Anita 'Baytins' O'Reilly (Laois)
John 'Fighting Cock' O'Connor (Carlow)
Eugene 'Ball Bag' Bell (Kerry)
Alan 'Shyte-hawk' Clarke (Wicklow)
Shane 'Bockshty' Smith (Leitrim)
Michael 'Aisy' White (Offaly)
Eileen 'Mopsey' Irish (Kerry)
Bernadette 'Skutch' Stackpoole (Clare)
J.P. 'Mr. Fed' Monaghan (Kilkenny)
Susie 'Agra-een' O'Malley (Meath / Roscommon)
Lorraine 'Scoby' McGrory (Louth)
Trevor 'Wheeze Choice' Eivers (Longford)
Catherine 'The Bibe' Evans (Waterford)

…most of all, thanks to all de udder eejits on d'Internet for submitting slang to www.slang.ie

Table of Contents

On reading the book 6

Introduction 7

The Basics 10

A Glossary of General Irish Slang 15

The 32 County Guide 22

Cork: The Rebels 23

Mayo: The Westerners 30

Sligo: Yeat's County 36

Waterford: The Déise 42

Tipperary: The Premier 48

Dublin: Metropolitans 54

Kilkenny: The Cats 60

Offaly: The Faithful 65

Wexford: Yellow-bellies 70

Galway: The Tribesmen 75

Cavan: The Breffni 80

Donegal: Tír Conaill 84

Carlow: Scallion Eaters 88

Antrim: The Glens 92

Limerick: Shannonsiders 96

Longford: O'Farrell County 100

Kerry: The Kingdom 103

Meath: The Royals 106

Armagh: The Orchard 109

Louth: The Wee County 113

Clare: The Banner 116

Kildare: The Lilywhites 119

Wicklow: The Garden 122

Fermanagh: Ernesiders 125

Laois: O' Moore County 128

Monaghan: The Farney 131

Leitrim: The Ridge 134

Westmeath: Lake County 137

Derry: Oak Leafs 140

Down: The Fortress 143

Roscommon: Sheepstealers 146

Tyrone: The Red Hands 149

About the Author 152

On reading the book

The order of the counties was determined by their placement on the **www.slang.ie** leader-board on the 18th Feb 2008. Counties that appear earlier have more entries, in proportion to the number of slang terms submitted over d'Internet.

Entries are arranged in alphabetical order under each county and are defined as follows:

Word (class, e.g. n. for noun)
Explanation of word

"Sample Usage"

e.g.

Hole (n.)
The posterior opening of the alimentary canal, through which the excrements are expelled.

*"When I get home I'm going to tear me wife's knickers off...
...'cos they're cuttin' de feckin' hole off me!!!"*

Word Classes:

n.	Noun
v.	Verb
adj.	Adjective
adv.	Adverb
exp.	Expression

For Focal Sake!

Introduction

"Well langer, what's de crack! I'm quare hungry boy. I'm so hungry I'd ate de balls off a low flyin' duck so I would. Let's make shapes and get a few rissoles lad, but not from dat hole we went to last time. I got sweat scald on me nawrse and had to put cream on me irey hole for a week 'cos of the dose of the skitters I got from aytin' in dayer. So anyways, let's head out on the lush after for a few scoops and get mahawng drunk an' den go buck-leppin' with the biys hiy! I fancy shiftin' wanna dem tome beurs dat are always bullin' for lads to lob de gob on 'em. Playse doh, no matter how much of a boodawn I get, don't let me feek de same wan as last time sham 'cos I woke up de next mornin' in a nawful sitch-ye-ashian. Me mouth was like an arab's tackie and me arm was stuck under some yungwan with a face like a well slapped arse."

If you can read the above paragraph, you're probably Irish. If not, you should be able to read it by the time you have finished this book. If you cannot wait until then it may be interpreted as follows...

"Hello there old chap? Have you any news pray tell? I am quite hungry my good fellow. The hunger has hit me so terribly that I would actually bite the testicles clean off a duck flying at a low altitude. Let us go immediately and get an arbitrary number of deep-fried, spicy, cake-shaped, savoury delights, however we must not purchase them from that poor

quality establishment we paid a visit to on the previous occasion. I got a very bad rash on the inner part of my posterior, and I had to apply cream to my extremely sensitive anus for an entire week, caused by a serious bout of diarrhoea that I acquired from ingesting at that particular eatery. In any case, let us go out on the town and overindulge on alcoholic beverages in order that we may become intoxicated beyond our physical and mental capacity, and following that we shall dance vigorously at some unknown venue with our fellow cohorts. I would very much like to pet with one of those extremely attractive ladies, so keen on males taking the liberty of kissing them profusely. Please though, no matter how sexually excited I get, do not let me romance the same individual that I did on the previous excursion, for when I woke up the next day I was in dire straits. I was left with an oral orifice that was as arid as an Arab's foot protection device, with my arm stuck under a lady with a countenance comparable to that of a chastised posterior!"

'For Focal Sake!' was compiled to capture and preserve the unique flavours of slang encountered across the 32 counties of Ireland. From my own early experiences, I realised that the accents and slang between the counties in South East Ireland differed dramatically. For example, Wexford people say "quare" instead of very, Tipperary people are obsessed with the word mickey, and Waterford people say "boy" at the end of every sentence. In my working life, as I met more and more people from around the country, I realised the level of diversity did not diminish as one went further a field. So, given my background in the software industry, I decided to use my skills to create a website, called **www.slang.ie**, in order to capture the various nuances of our "mudder tongue." Within a matter of months there were literally thousands of entries added to it by people from the 32 counties of Ireland. As a result, I decided to compile this book through a process of cross checking the entries submitted over d'Internet with my own research, and through talking with people from as many counties as possible.

The book is entitled 'For Focal Sake!' as it was put together for the sake of words (focal being the Gaelic for word). Ireland's dialects will most likely merge over time, especially in this, the information age. Perhaps this book will act as a checkpoint in time for future generations to look back at how we "useta spayke."

Says you: *"Enough of d'oul bollox, go an' have yer shyte ye big eejit and get on with it!"*

OK, hould yer whisht for wan second. Without further ado, here it is, the very first 32-County Guide to Irish Slang: **'For Focal Sake!'**

The Basics

If for some reason you are unfamiliar with Irish slang, the following section provides a quick overview of the basics to get you through the somewhat rough terrain that constitutes the book.

Lesson wan: counting

One, two, three, four, five becomes…
Wan (All), tew (South East), tree (All), fower (South), fiyev (East), schickshe (West), sebm (North), eigh (Midlands) niyen (East), tin (South West), 'levin (All), twellev (South), turteen (All), fowerteen (South), fufteen (North) etc.

Lesson tew: ee to ay

Words with a strong 'e' sound are often pronounced with a strong 'a' sound. For example, tea become tay etc.

Lesson tree: ol to oul

Words that contain the strong 'o' sound change to an 'au' sound (like ow). For example, old becomes ould (often with the 'd' dropped) and breakfast-roll becomes breakfast-roul.

Lesson fower: extra syllable

Many counties add an extra syllable to words with long vowel sounds. Depending on the word a 'w' or 'y' is added. For example, school and ride become schoowel and riyed.

Lesson fiyev: dropped ts and ds

This rule applies to words where a t or d in the middle of a word is replaced with an 'h' sound or is just completely dropped. The severity of this rule changes as you move around the country. A good example of this would be in the midlands where a popular brand of packet snack, called Tayto, is pronounced Tay-ho.

Lesson schickshe: the 'th' rule

It is genetically impossible for people in Ireland to pronounce words starting with 'th' correctly. A rhyme taught at school to try overcome this problem goes something like:

"This, that, these and those, that's the way the T-H goes!"

However its futility is only fully realised when teachers hear the whole class shouting:

"Dis, dat, deese, and doze, das de way de T-H goes!"

Some words that begin with 'th' are pronounced with a strong 't' sound rather than a 'd' sound as above e.g. "That thing over there" would translate as, "Dat **t**ing over dayer."

The 'th' rule also applies within words and at the end of words. For example other, is pronounced udder and bath is pronounced bat.

Lesson sebm: the guttural r

In some counties in the midlands and south e.g. Limerick, Kerry, Tipperary, Cork, Waterford the 'r' sound can be pronounced almost as a 'gh' sound. For example, 'true' become 'tghue.' Some suggest this is French in origin.

Lesson eigh': from me to you

Irish people never say "my" or "you," instead they say "me" and "ye" respectively. For example, "Ah come on boy, gimme back me Rick Astley tape? Ye have it since 1987!"

Lesson niyen: dooby dooby doo

"Do be," translates directly as "is" or "are." For example, if someone's hands are always dirty, one could say, "His hands do be manky!"

Lesson tin: 'tis, d'oul, g'wan

When short words such as "it," "the" and "go" appear before words, they are abbreviated and joined with the word. For example if "it" precedes "is" or "was" they combine to become 'tis and 'twas. For example:

boy: *"'twas your go last time, now 'tis my go."*
girl: *"'tisn't."*
boy: *"'tis."* Ad infinitum…

If "go" precedes "on" they combine to become g'wan and it gets even more complicated when "the" appears before words that start with a vowel, as the 'th' rule is also invoked. For example, "the Internet" becomes d'Internet.

Lesson 'levin: arra

Arra is generally used when someone is looking on the bright side after something bad has happened. For example, "Arra, de lessons are nayrley finished." "Yerra" and "erra" can also be used instead of "arra" and are derived from the Irish word "dhera," pronounced yerra.

Lesson twellev: yer wan / man

Yer wan / man is used to point out a person one does not know. For example, "look at the head of yer wan!" "Yer" directly translates to "your." To insult someone, one could simply use the expression, "Yer mudder!"

Lesson turteen: drunken focal

Irish people have a huge variety of adjectives to describe the various stages of drunken intoxication. When they go on a "session" (a night of merriment involving alcohol), the following words might describe the resultant state: blithero, blocked, blootered, blotto, bollock drunk, buckled, bunched, flamin', flootered, full as a bingo bus, gally-bandered, gee-eyed, in bits, in da (divine) horrors, in de baloobas, in de mowldies, in ribbons, in the gizoolies, in the rats, langered, langers, locked (out of me tree), mahawng, merry, mowldy, ossified, paralatic, pissed as a fart, plastered, polluted, rat-arsed, schteamed, scuttered, sloshed, steamboats, sozzled, stotious, twisted, wasted, well-oiled and wrote off etc. and that's just to get started!!!

Lesson fowerteen: as full as

Irish people are obsessed with similes and analogies… one is never just hungry or full, they are so hungry, they'd "ate the back door buttered," or they are so full, they're "as full as a tinker's tit!" Examples of this can be found throughout this book.

Lesson fufteen: Norn Ayern

Northern Ireland is called Norn Ayern by its own inhabitants. Therefore, as a mark of respect, it will be referred to as Norn Ayern for the remainder of this book. There are many not-so-subtle differences between Norn Ayern's and Southern Ireland's slang. Some of these differences include:

- putting "hiy" at the end of every sentence
- saying thur instead of there
- saying aye instead of yes
- saying ach instead of ah!
- saying wee instead of small
- saying thon instead of that
- saying boke instead of puke
- saying get instead of git
- pronouncing short 'o' sounds as 'a' sounds e.g. job = jab, bollix = ballix
- pronouncing 's' as 'sh' e.g. arse = awrshe
- elongating short 'a' sounds e.g. understand becomes underschtawnd
- overuse of the word 'situation' and pronouncing it 'sitch-ye-ashian'

A Glossary of General Irish Slang

The following section gives a brief overview of some of the most common slang terms used throughout Ireland. This should equip the unfamiliar reader with enough vocabulary to make sense of the rest of the book.

Anudder: Someone or something else. Not to be confused with the bovine glandular organ, in which milk is stored and secreted. The popular Irish song, 'I useta love her' contains the lyrics "I have fallen for anudder," which does not refer to some weird cow fetish.

Arse: One's posterior. The 'r' is pronounced very definitely. In Northern counties it is pronounced awrshe.

Box / Dig: A punch. If a person of questionable upbringing is in one's face, an appropriate phrase to remove them from one's presence might be, "Feck off or I'll box de feckin' head off ya!"

Bollix: Can be used to refer to the male testes and scrotum collectively. Can also be used as an affectionate term for a male friend, as in "g'wan ye bollix." If spelt with an 'ox' it can refer to a person with whom one is totally dissatisfied, such as a "biased, blind, baldy, boll**ox** of a ref!"

Crack: Slang word for fun, involving alcohol and music. Craic, the gaelicized version is often labelled as *faux*-Irish as it is not "real" Irish per se.

The term is said to originate from Scotland and has been adopted throughout the whole of Ireland without exception. Often used in a greeting as in "What's the craic?"

Culchie: Someone from the countryside, which to the Dubs is anyone living outside Dublin city. Other general terms to describe culchies include bog-warrior (bogger) and muck-savage.

Cuncha: A person with whom one is dissatisfied. For example, "Ye farted again ye dirty bollix, watcha do dat for ye cuncha?"

Diddies: Childish term for mammary glands / breasts. Can refer to man boobs (moobs) also.

Eejit / Feckin' Eejit: Probably the most overused Irish word, means idiot. Most often used in a derogatory sense. For example, "Ye big half-shit feckin' eejit!"

Fanny: The outward facing part of the female reproductive organ. Often causes problems for the Irish when visiting the USA, as fanny translates as arse across the big pond.

Feck: A non-vulgar replacement for a similar word with a 'u' instead of the 'e'. Like eejit, it is used extensively. Does not have any sexual connotations, i.e. one would not say "I'd like to feck yer wan." However, it can be used in most other circumstances. For example, "feck dat," "feck off," "I will in me feckin' hole!" etc.

For Focal Sake!

Gas: Used to describe someone or something that was funny. For example, "it was a gas crack" or "he's a gas man."

Gawk: To look at someone or something. For example "What are you gawkin' at?"

Gee: See Fanny. Often used as the focal point (no pun intended) of a sarcastic response by a female, e.g. "I will in me Jimmy Magee!"

Gowl: See Fanny. Can also describe the act of horseplay or a person one does not like. For example, "Give up the gowling ye gowl!"

Gobshyte, Gobsheen, Gobdaw, Gombeen: See eejit. Incidentally, gob means mouth.

Gurrier: A yungfella up to no good, sometimes called a tipper or guyer.

Handy: Easy, as in "take it handy," or good, as in "he's a handy hurler!"

Hole / Hoop: The posterior opening of the alimentary canal. Used extensively, for example, "a boot in de hole" means a kick in the posterior; and "did you get your hole?" questions whether one pulled; finally, "I will in my hole" means someone will not do what you asked of them. Hoop is becoming a popular alternative to hole in modern Ireland.

Hoor: Literally the Irish pronunciation of whore, but is generally used in an affectionate manner. For example "He's a cute-hoor / hairy-hoor / hoor's boot" etc.

Jacks: The toilet or W.C. Comes from Shakespeare's King Lear (II ii 74-6), "I shall tread this unbolted villain into mortar, and daub the wall of a jakes with him."

Jayney Mack, Jaykers, Jaypers: Expressions of surprise, probably to stop individuals from taking the Lord's name in vain.

Jaysis/Jaysus: Irish pronunciation of Jesus.

Jonnies: Contraceptive devices, often called rubber Jonnies.

Knackered: To be extremely tired. It comes from the original meaning of the word Knacker and not the modern derogatory term for a member of the travelling community.

Mudder: Irish pronunciation of mother. Often used in an insulting manner i.e. "Yer Mudder!"

Neck like a Jockey's dickie / bollix: Someone that is extroverted and will chance anything. A "chancer" or a "cute hoor" would have a neck like a jockey's dickie i.e. pushy and thick skinned.

Nah: No.

Nob / Knob: A childish name for the male appendage, can be used in a similar way to gee to vehemently say no to somebody e.g. "I will in me corn on de cob!"

Mineral / Mingrel: A small bottle of a carbonated drink usually given free with a bag of chips and a battered sausage in chippers.

For Focal Sake!

Oxter: The armpit. If one smelled like a Donkey's oxter, they would be quite smelly indeed.

Press: A cupboard. One puts delph (plates, cups and saucers) in a press.

Piss: Adult term for urine, if one goes on the piss one is heading out for a few beverages with their friends. In the USA pissed means annoyed, however in Ireland it means drunk.

Rubber: An eraser, usually found in a pencil case with rulers and toppers. Can also mean condom (see Jonnies).

Runners: Training shoes. In the UK runners are called trainers; in the US they're called sneakers; in Cork they're called rubber dollies; in Limerick, tackies; in Norn Ayern, gutties; and in Kerry, buffers.

Root / Boot: A terrible kick, if one received a "root in de hole" it would be very sore indeed.

Sack / Balls: A childish term for one's scrotum. Nob and sack go hand in hand. A less offensive term for one's sack is the Gaelic for balls, líathróidí (pronounced lee rhodey). "Bite me sack!" is a vulgar phrase often used today in place of "Feck off!"

Sangwich, Sanwich, Sammich, Samwidge: Common mispronunciations of the word sandwich. Sammwidges are normally accompanied by a cuppa tay.

Shat: To defecate, past tense. Often used in a metaphorical sense e.g. "When she said she'd shift me, I nearly shat meself!"

Shyte: Literally means excrement. Can be used in various circumstances e.g. if one is disappointed they might shout, "ah shyte on it anyway" or if one is displeased with another they might say "go an' have yer shyte!"

Shift: Generally means to enthusiastically kiss a member of the opposite sex. Can mean quite a bit more than kissing in some counties. Examples of other words for shifting such as meetin' and tippin' can be found throughout this book.

Slug: A mouthful of any given beverage.

Sliced Pan: A sliced loaf of bread. On either end of a sliced pan you will find the heel.

Scanger: A derogatory term for a track-suit wearing individual with a questionable upbringing. The male variety can often be identified easily by the trade-mark eyebrow on upper lip syndrome. The Norn Ayern equivalent is spide / steek, the British equivalent is chav, and US equivalent is trailer-trash.

Skint: To be without any money.

Shades: The Garda (Irish Police Force).

Sound: A person who is liked because they do nice things for their friends e.g. "Paddy gave me a loand of hees car. He's sound as a trout!"

For Focal Sake!

Tay: Tea as pronounced by the Irish, comes from the Gaelic word tae, pronounced tay.

Tayto: Tayto is an Irish brand of potato chip and corn packet snack. As with Hoover and vacuum cleaners, Tayto has become synonymous with any type of savoury packet snack in many parts of the country.

Topper: A pencil shearer or sharpener.

Tool: Another word for an eejit. Spanner and spoon are other alternatives.

Wan: A female individual often preceded with yer, yung or oul.

Wee-Wee: Childish term for urine. 'Stop de bus we want a wee wew,' is an old tour bus favourite sung to the tune of 'Glory, Glory Hallelujah.' This sort of stop on a bus journey is known throughout the country as a piss-stop.

Well: A greeting used in many counties throughout the country often used in conjunction with "girl" or "boy."

Yoke: An arbitrary object, can also be used to refer to a person as in, "Ye mad yoke!"

Yungwan / Yungfella: Young female / male. Yungwans and yungfellas do be always shifting wan anudder.

The 32 County Guide

Now that you are equipped with the vocabulary and lessons from the previous chapter, the rest of the book should be "no bodder" to you!

As stated previously, the order of the counties in the book was determined by their placement on the **www.slang.ie** leader-board on the 18th February 2008. Counties that appear earlier have more entries in proportion to the amount accumulated on d'Internet.

NOTE: If you feel that important entries are missing from the book, you might consider logging on to d'Internet and signing up to **www.slang.ie** today. This will ensure that your county is represented properly online and in future publications and revisions of this book. Once you have signed up and log in, you can post new and rate existing slang entries. Every entry counts and it will help preserve your county's slang for future generations.

G'wan, g'wan, g'wan, g'wan, g'wan…

Sign up to **www.slang.ie** today and give a focal about your county.

For Focal Sake!

Cork: The Rebels

As Gaeilge: Corcaigh (Bog / Marsh)
Province: Munster
County Town: Cork City
Known as: The Rebel County
Nickname: The Rebels, The Langers
The Donkey Aters
Colours: Red & White
Song: The banks of my own lovely Lee
Funny Places: Cannawee, Ringaskiddy, Gaggin, Titeskin

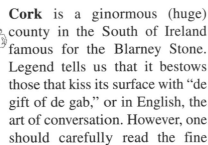

Cork is a ginormous (huge) county in the South of Ireland famous for the Blarney Stone. Legend tells us that it bestows those that kiss its surface with "de gift of de gab," or in English, the art of conversation. However, one should carefully read the fine etchings before kissing this magical stone as one of the possible side effects one may suffer from is the erratically pitched Cork accent, which is regarded as one of the most bizarre in Ireland. Cork is also famous for its scenic coast-line, its vibrant City, and its strong hurling and football tradition and, well... quite simply... langers.

Note: If someone from Cork calls you Timmy, as in "c'mere Timmy", do not be alarmed, they are simply asking you to go over to them.

Alri biy (exp.)

A form of greeting. Can mean okay or "hello young fellow."

"Alri biy! Is it yourself that is in it?"

Bazz (v.)

A collection or mass of filaments growing from the skin in the pubic area. Pubic hair.

"Das de hairiest fanta bazz I've ever seen! Did yer mudder knit dat for ya like?"

Boodawn (n.)

The male appendage. Usually this term is used to describe it in an excited state.

"I only have to look at the aul doll an' I get such a boodawn you could bayte an ass out of a bog with it!"

Bull, Bullin', Bulled (v.)

Slang used by countrymen / construction workers to describe the act of copulation.

"I'd love to bull her / she's bullin' for it / I bulled her last night etc."

Craw Sick (exp.)

Sick or nauseous to the point that vomiting becomes inevitable.

"Jaypers, I'm craw sick dis mornin' like after dem bottles of stout la!"

For Focal Sake!

Dowcha boy (exp.)

An expression used to enthusiastically praise an individual, usually at GAA matches. Similar to "honyabiya."

"Das it boy, stick it in the back of the net like... Dowcha boy!"

Fla (n.)

A good looking person. Can also mean sexual intercourse.

"Jay yer wan is a right fla, unlike her sister who has a face like a well slapped arse!"

Fifty-Fifty (n.)

A date.

"I went on a fifty-fifty last night but 'twas more like a fifty 'cos I ended up being short changed... the bibe never showed up like!"

Gobblejob (n.)

Fellatio.

"I hear yer wan gives out gobblejobs goodo!"

Honyabiya (exp.)

Shouted uncontrollably by fans at GAA matches when a player gets a good score.

"Straight over the black spot, honyabiya!"

I will yeah (exp.)

Sarcastic expression, used to tell someone that you will not perform the requested task.

"Give you a gobblejob? I will yeah!"

Jack's Hole (exp.)

The Jack Lynch Tunnel. Not to be confused with the beach with the same name in Co. Wicklow.

"I was stuck in Jack's hole for an hour yesterday... with the traffic."

Jaggin' (n.)

Seeing someone.

Rebel: *"I'm tellin' ye la, I'm jaggin' dat beur that lives up the road..."*

Langer: *"I'd say jaggen' her is like throwin' a cocktail sausage down Patrick Street!"*

Langer (n.)

Literally means penis, but can be used as an insult, or to affectionately refer to Cork people. It is a very flexible word and can be used in several situations.

"Ye langer! Ye made me drink a langer-load and now I'm langers, ye langball!"

For Focal Sake!

Like (n.)
Used at the end of every sentence. Can sometimes be used at the start of sentences too.

"Like eh, I asked me oul doll for a gobblejob and it went down like a cup of cold sick!"

La (n.)
An abbreviation of lad.

"Here la, there la, look la, howaya la etc."

Lob the gob (exp.)
An expression used to describe the initiation of a passionate kiss, often without the permission of the gobbee (see Throw the head in, Louth).

"I'm gonta bayte de head offa dat lang, did ye see de bollix lob de gob on me oul flower!"

Manky (exp.)
Filthy dirty.

"Jay biddy, if yer goin' in to get a Brazilian ye better give yer manky bazz a good scrubbin'!"

Noodenaw (n.)
A dope or eejit, pronounced newt-nah elsehwere.

"He's some noodenaw, he's about as useful as a Kerryman with a hurley!"

Oul Doll (exp.)

Term used to describe a girlfriend or female spouse... can refer to ones mother in other counties which can lead to serious confusion. Oul Fella means dad, Oul Pair means parents and Oul Stock means friend.

Rebel: *"Did ya shift yer oul doll last night?"*

Monaghonian: *"Yer sick ye dirty langer!"*

Poxed (n.)

As lucky as feck.

"Yer man is poxed like... he'd sell mice at a crossroads so he would!"

Poppies(n.)

Potatoes.

"Ma, are ye puttin' de poppies on or wha' like? I'm so hungry I'd ate a scabby cat!"

Rubber Dollies (n.)

Training shoes or runners.

"Look at de state of the tatty rubber dollies on yer man, he's so mayne he could peel an orange in his pocket with boxing gloves on!"

[**see also:** tackies: Limerick, gutties: Antrim]

Read de hole off (exp.)
To give out about someone behind their back.

"She read de hole off yer wan about her red irey hole!"

Relax de cacks (exp.)
An instruction to tell someone to chill out.

"Relax de cacks boy an' take a chill pill…"

Tayties (n.)
See poppies.

The People's Republic of Cork (n.)
Cork people believe they live in their own independent state… It suits the rest of the country though as it keeps the weird accent from spreading too far past the boundary.

Wazzie (n.)
A wasp.

"Maa, will ye kill dat wazzie for me, it's like Tommy Walsh in his Kilkenny jersey, he won't get off me back!"

Mayo: The Westerners

As Gaeilge: Maigh Eo
(Plain of the Yews)
Province: Connacht
County Town: Castlebar
Known as: The Yew / Heather /
Maritime County
Nickname: The Westerners
Colours: Green & Red
Song: Moonlight on Mayo, The Boys
from the County Mayo
Funny Places: Cong, Knock, Pontoon

Mayo (pronounced M'yoh by the locals) is located in the Wesht. Contrary to popular belief, Mayo is not where the white creamy dressing with the same name comes from, though it is used extensively in the local chippers there. The town of Cong was the location a famous film (no, not the one about the giant ape) entitled 'The Quiet Man.' Mayo is a very spiritual county as people from all over the world go on pilgrimage to Croagh Patrick. This is the site where St. Patrick not only drove snakes from Ireland, but all fossilised traces of them too. Then there's Knock, where a verified apparition occurred and a massive international airport set up to cash in on this good fortune.

For Focal Sake!

Annaconya (n.)

A very large poo resembling a large South-American snake.

"Run sham, I'm after layvin' a mawsive annaconya in the jawx an' 'tis blocked up!"

Ah Bo (exp.)

An expression to stress something is the truth.

"Ah bo, yer de finesht beek I ever saw, I have a pain in me belly with love for ya!"

Arra Musha (exp.)

Arra can be used on its own to express apathy. Musha is used to augment the arra.

"Waa-whoo, did you see de mawtch?"
"Arra musha, twas pure conya!"

Away for Slates (exp.)

Means on the pigs back, sorted.

"He's away for slates now he's won de lotto."

Bawdrig Bio (exp.)

Legendary school yard chant roared before beatings were dished out by bullies. The chant starts at a low decibel level and crescendos louder and louder until the kicks and thumps start, until a final *"Bawdrig Bawdrig Bawdrig Bio"* is expelled in a synchronous tribal scream from the mouths of the baytin' dishers outers.

Beek (n.)

A fine looking lady, beekage being the plural.

"Soonie feenóg, beekage at 3 O'Clock!"

Bogdized (adj.)

Someone who has lived in the countryside amongst bog warriors for far too long.

"Yer bogdized from living in de schticks!"

Boul Feen / Wan (n.)

One's father / mother.

"Yer good feenóg, but 'tis not off a stone ye licked it, yer boul feen was a legend."

Butt on de Butta de Lug (exp.)

A belt across the face, just under the ear.

"Shup or you'll get a butt on de butta de lug!"

Covies & Fish-heads (n.)

Nicknames for Westport and Castlebar people respectively.

"Whatever you do, don't put the Covies and Fish-heads together or there'll be trouble!!!"

Feenóg (n.)

A young man.

"Yer man's feenóg is only 4 and even he'd do better than those thick nucks!"

For Focal Sake!

Fermanagh Banana (n.)

A wild football bulltoe shot that invariably goes miles wide. Legend has it that the technique was perfected in Fermanagh.

"Yer man gave it holly and produced a Fermanagh banana, we're steeped!"

Gollumned (exp.)

The activity of pulling bed clothes from a sleeping skinny person.

"The poor feen got gollumned at the party!"

Jaunter (n.)

A bike, but the word jaunt can be used to describe a ride, or sexual intercourse.

"If that gowdger asks me to jaunt I'm gonna open him like a bag a Tayho! I'll give him so many thumps he'll be begging for a kick!"

Hong (n.)

A very bad smell indeed. I wonder is there a hong in Cong?

"Arra would you keep that nawrse under control? There's a hong of conya in here now because of that last nawrt ye left off!"

Lorc (n.)

An automobile.

"Waa-whoo... Fancy a jaunt in me lorc?"

Lush (n.)

Alcoholic beverages. Lushed describes the inebriated state after too many lushes.

"People call me a lusher just 'cos I am lushed on black milkshakes (stout) all the time!!!"

Me Velvet Purse (n.)

The male scrotum or bollix.

"Dat meek gave me a 'nawful boot in de velvet purse when I asked her to jaunt."

Meek (n.)

A pretty enough looking girl but not quite a beek and definitely not a feek (see Galway).

"Happy are the meek for they will be jaunted!"

Mighty (n.)

A very popular word used in the Wesht used instead of great.

"Jay lad, 'twash a mighty crack altogether!"

Nawrse (n.)

The posterior or arse as it is known in Éire.

"Biddy, dat feen has a mighty nawrse on him!"

Note: It is common in Mayo to replace the starting letter of some words with 'n,' some examples include: nurp (burp), nawrt (fart), nawrved (starved) etc.

For Focal Sake!

Nucking (adv.)

The act of kissing the head off someone.

"I caught you nucking de head offa some tome beek… Fair play feenog!"

Note: Nuck literally translates as head and is used in many circumstances. For example: off their nuck (crazy), pig's nuck (ugly head), upside down nuck (bald man with a beard), crusty nuck (of new age tendencies), gugg nuck (baldy head), froshty nuck (pale face), turbo nuck (huge head), bird nuck (big nose) etc.

Soonie (v.)

An instruction to look at something.

"Soonie, look at the nawrse on dat beek!"

Schweat Schkald (n.)

Rash around inner thighs and nawrse area. Known as Ire in some other counties.

"I cawn't play cos have a dose of schweat schkald around de hoop of me nawrse!"

Waa-whoo (n.)

A greeting unique to County Mayo.

"Waa-whoo mate how's de crack!"
"Yip ya biya, the crack is ninety!"

Sligo: Yeat's County

As Gaeilge: Sligeach (Shell River)
Province: Connacht
County Town: Sligo
Known as: Yeat's County
Nickname: Herring Pickers, Magpies
Colours: Black & White
Song: The Isle of Innisfree, Down By The Sally Gardens
Funny Places: Tubbercurry, Doomore

Sligo is wedged in between Mayo, Roscommon and Leitrim on the North West Coast. Sligo has had a profound effect on two magnificent writers: William Butler Yeats and Bram Stoker. W.B. Yeats was born and reared in Sligo and often romanticised about the beauty of the county in his literary works. Bram Stoker was the son of a Sligo woman and her stories about the Cholera epidemic of 1832 are said to have inspired his dark writings in the Dracula novel. Sligo harbour features a giant Metalman perched on a 15 foot base at Rosses Point. Some say he is one of 4 originals. One of the others can be found in Tramore, Co. Waterford, but the other two must have gone AWOL, just like yer man from Westlife… arra, he wasn't from Sligo anyway.

For Focal Sake!

Adlam (v.)
An eejit in the old tongue.

"He ducked (snuck) off on me at the bar and left me holdin' two pints like a right gomie adlam."

Buckleppin (v.)
The mad acts of a person who is overly excited in a disco / nightclub. Also known as jigacting.

"Arra sher here, ye were buckled after the Buckies and ended up buckleppin round Envy City (Envy night club or Equinox as it used to be known) last night like a mad yoke!"

Cert (adj.)
Most definitely.

"Would you be with (shift) me sister?"
"Cert, I would boy!"

Come 'round to yerself (adj.)
Most certainly not. Think again.

"Givvus a lush of yer Bucky (see Armagh)?"
"Come 'round to yerself ye loother!"

Columba's (n.)
The Mental Hospital.

"Ah lawds I can't lush any more or I'll end up in Columba's or the Leitrim Hotel"

Doggin' Into (n.)

A term used to describe a couple that are enthusiastically petting each other in full view. Can also be used to describe getting into something else like food, GAA match etc.

"Do you see you do ya, ya dirtbox? If I catch you doggin' into yer dolly while I'm doggin' into me dinner again I'll burst ya!"

Ellbow (exp.)

A greeting of sorts. A bastardisation of the phrase "Well boy" in Sligonian. Over time the 'w' in well was dropped and the boy evolved into an 'oh' sound.

"Ellbow, ow's she cutting?'
"Ah biy, up de middle an' down de sides!"

Finer (n.)

An extremely attractive individual.

"He's a finer, so he is. I would, so I would!"

Header (n.)

An affectionate term for someone that's a little bit mental or that acts on a whim. Probably an abbreviated version of "head-the-ball."

"He's a wee header so he is! He's always fighting with his dolly outside the Four Lights (referring to a famous chipper in Sligo)."

In the boat (exp.)

To be infatuated with someone.

"Oh girls I'm soo in de boat with yer man dat works in the Four Lights, de Jimmy burgers he makes are just mighty!!!"

Lush Head (n.)

A term used to describe someone that overindulges with alcoholic beverages.

"Surprise, surprise, the lush heads are out minker drinkin' again tonight!"

Loother (n.)

Variation of Looder, which is an abbreviation of Liúdramán (Gaelic for a useless eejit).

"The thunderin' loother dropped the ball again, I must be off me box putting him on!!!"

Mink(er) (n.)

A disreputable person.

"I caught de dirty minker robbing knickerses off the nuns line again! Ah now!"

[**see also:** gurrier]

Mint (n.)

Something extremely good.

"Did ya see his new yoke, 'tis mint!"

Pure Dry (exp.)

A term used to describe a person or situation that is overly boring.

"He's a cat (see Armagh / Waterford) teacher... he's pure dry altogether!"

Right Shammer (exp.)

A greeting for a male friend often used by Minkers. Short for "are you alright sham?"

"'Right Shammer how's de hammer???"
"Fulla juice and ready for use!"

Roaster (exp.)

Someone of an agricultural persuasion.

"Peace Park is fulla roasters today lawds!"

Score (v.)

To shift someone.

Yungfella: *"Did you score?"*
Yungwan: *"I did yeah!"* i.e. no feckin' way
Yungfella: *"Ah now, you're in a bould mood, who lit de fuse on your tampon?"*

Shogies (n.)

Home of Sligo Rovers F.C.

"I better make a bursht lawds, I'm headin to de Shogies to watch us bayte de Town!"
"Schtall up an' I'll head with you."

For Focal Sake!

Sight (adj.)

A lot of a particular substance in Sligonian.

"Jay yer lookin well, you've lost a sight of weight yungfella, haven't you?"

Skillage (n.)

Someone who has great skill in a particular discipline.

"He buried it in de back of the net, pure skillage in the village lawds!"

Unreal / Unnatural (adv.)

Simple replacement words for unbelievable.

"Lads de sesh was unreal last night, I'm as sick as de plane to Lourdes dis morning an' I have an unnatural headache!"

Virgin Megastore (n.)

Nickname for the Mercy Convent.

Yungfella1: *"Dem youngwans in de Virgin Megastore are a pack of pure dry, moany, wreck de heads."*

Yungfella2, in agreement, mutters: *"Ahoii!"*

Waterford: The Déise

As Gaeilge: Port Láirge
                    (Leg Shaped River)
Province: Munster
County Town: Dungarvan
Known as: The Gentle / Crystal County
Nickname: The Déise (Decies) / Blaas
Colours: White & Blue
Song: Do bhios-sa lá i bPort Láirge,
               Happy Moments
Funny Places: Kilmacbogey, Ring, Gaul

 **Waterford** is located on the South East coast and is famed for its world class crystal. Waterford City, the oldest city in Ireland, is the place where the Irish flag was first flown (by T. F. Meagher). Waterfordians are collectively known as the Déise, as many moons ago a tribe of the same name got focalled out of Tara, Co. Meath, and settled in what we now know as Waterford. Waterford people like nothing better than to drink large bottles of stout off the shelf before heading to the chipper for a fayde of scallops. The people are often called blaas as there is a local bread product with the same name. Waterford gave the world the rasher and ETS Walton was the first man to split the atom. Wonder who was first to split the blaa?

For Focal Sake!

Anwell (adv.)

Without question and beyond doubt.

*"G'waffwit (shift) yer sister for a few blaas???
Anwell I would boy!"*

Blaa (n.)

A floury square bread roll of sorts, in one of three
varieties: soft, crusty or chewy. The blaa is a
culinary delight, unique to Waterford.

*"Mammy... put loads of red lead in me blaa today,
dayer wahent a bit in it yesterday an' I was
shakin' like a shittin' dog in class!"*

Baythur (n.)

A unpleasant looking female, so large that she
could kick-start a combine harvester.

*"She's some baythur boy! I'd rather wake up next
to a Bilberry goat den her so I would!!!"*

Cannt (v.)

The act of losing the central playing apparatus of
a game without possibility of retrieval.

"What did you cannt de ball for ye bollix?"

Cat Malojan (adj.)

Having undesirable or negative qualities. Cat is
also used in Armagh / Sligo and other areas.

*"Dat owl ghrroad to Kilkenny is cat dog malojan!
Tank feck we're getting a new wan!"*

Chynies (n.)

Small spherical pieces made of marble, glass etc., and used as a plaything by children.

"I got some dose o' piles boy. Dey were like a big bag a chynies!"

Das De Why / How (exp.)

That is just the way things are.

Mickey: *"But why Daddy?"*
Daddy: *"Cos das de why!"*

Doonchy (adj.)

Extremely small. Mass challenged.

Yer wan had deese doonchy diddies boy! Dey looked like tablets on an ironin' board boy!

Fungarvan (n.)

An affectionate term for Dungarvan.

"Are ye headin' down tew Fraher Field in Fungarvan for de auld match?"

Gallybander (n.)

A home made slingshot/catapult, made out of a coat hanger and a mixed array of elastic bands. Can refer to an elastic band in the singular.

"I got a slap in de eye offa copper bullet fired from me brudder's gallybander and I couldn't see me blaas for a week!"

For Focal Sake!

Ire (n., pronounced eye-er)

A rash induced by rubbing together of skin and wet clothing on the inner thighs / buttocks.

"Yer man must have ire under his arms, his pants are so far up his hole!"

[**see also:** schweat schkald: Mayo]

Knucks (n.)

Small star shaped metal objects used in a game with the same name. Knucks were obtained from in the Ighrron Foundaghrree. Knucks can also be used as a euphemism for testicles.

"Look at the big set of knucks on yer man!!!"

Lack (n.)

Colloquial term for a female companion.

"Giz a layarge bohhel offa de shellef boy, anna Ritz for de lack!"

Make Shapes (exp)

To leave a person's company.

"Are ye right? I have to make shapes! De mudders after buyin' a fayde o' scallops!"

On de Ball (exp.)

An expression of agreement

"On de ball boy, spot on no bodder!"

On-real (exp.)

Something that is absolutely fantastic.

"The Déise were on-real yesterday boy!"

Ou'witchya! (exp.)

If a friend says that they are ou'withchya (out with you) then they mean they are no longer your friend. Preceding the phrase with blackspoh (black spot) is even more serious.

"Ye robbed me bag a' cans ye bollix, I'm blackspoh ou'withca now ye cuncha!"

Red Lead (n.)

A large, illuminous (sic), pink, meat-like sausage of unknown origin, otherwise known as luncheon sausage. Some say it is of a supernatural or extraterrestrial origin given its unusual colour and taste. Waterford locals believe it to be the original and best filling for blaas. Also goes by the name baloney in the West.

Scallop (n.)

A thick potato-slice, coated in batter and deep fried. Available in all good chippers around Waterford. A chipper of noteworthiness will also throw in a handful of chips for free.

"Do you want scallops with yer salt and vinegar boy!"

For Focal Sake!

Shellakybooky (n.)

Any of numerous aquatic (Perry Winkle) or terrestrial (Snail) molluscs, typically having a spirally coiled shell. A Snail.

"Shellaky Shellakybooky, stick out your horns and see the white lady coming to call you."

Smell off yer lack boy (exp.)

Probably the worst insult you can give a yungfella and will almost certainly lead to one getting "their go"... an appropriate response to the expression might be "Yer mudder!"

Tenna Past (n.)

Ten past the hour.

Mickey Mahon: *"What time is the bus due?"*
Tullamore Jew: *"Tenna past tew ye Blaa!"*

Wilnots (n.)

An entanglement in the "barse" region i.e. the area between one's balls and arse.

"Dem wilnots just will not come loose!"

Yer Go (v.)

Hand to hand combat.

"Do ya want yer go boy? I'll give ye a baytin' by de clock tower at tenna past 4! By the way, if I'm late feel free tew start without me!"

Tipperary: The Premier

As Gaeilge: Tiobraid Árann
                 (Well on the River)
Province: Munster
County Town: Clonmel, Nenagh
Known as: The Premier County
Nickname: The Stone Throwers, Tipp
Colours: Blue and Gold
Song: Slievenamon
Funny Places: Poulmucka (Pigs Hole), Horse &
                 Jockey, Nodstown

Tipperary (or Tipp) is a county, correction, two counties (North & South), located in the South. Tipp is famous for many things: cider, the Rock of Cashel, Cahir Castle, cider, horse breeding and beautiful fertile countryside, but more than all of this, it is famous for the Mecca of Hurling, Thurles, oh, and did I mention cider? Every year during the summer, this otherwise normal town is inundated with hang sangwich ating, tay drinking hurling fans out supporting their native counties. The square in Thurles, where the GAA was born, becomes the capital of Munster for those few days. A lesser known fact about Tipp is that Einstein's theory of relativity was proven beyond doubt by a strange property of Tipperary, i.e. no matter where you are, it is always a long way away.

For Focal Sake!

A Jump (exp.)

Sexual intimacy.

"'Ell biy, ye were wearin' de head off yer wan last night, did you get a jump after?"

Crut (adj.)

Common decency or sense.

"Dare's no crut to dat bollox!"

Can I've Arse on da? (exp.)

May I have the last sup of your can / bite of your bar / drag of your cigarette.

"Yungwan... can I've arse on dat fag?"

Clayned him out of it? (exp.)

To out mark / play one's opponent.

"He clayned de full back out of it every time the ball dropped in!"

Cheeps (n.)

The term used for French fries in Ballyporeen

"Lets go down chipper to get de cheeps."

Crayter (n.)

A term of endearment for a child. Can be used with poor to describe someone unfortunate.

"De poor crayter was on'y saturated!"

De Nashnist (n.)
The Nationalist newspaper

"Will ya get de nashnist with de messages?"

Drink a Farm (exp.)
To drink a copious amount, especially alcohol.

"I was dyin' o' de drute so I drunk a farm!"

Face like a blind cobbler's thumb
Someone so ugly, that they were not only hit by the ugly stick, the whole tree fell on them.

"Did you get a jump of de fella with de face like a blind cobbler's thumb?"

Fong it (v.)
The throw or pass something with vigour. One may give something fong.

"G'wan de premier, fong it would ye!"

Full as an Egg/Goose (exp.)
Had enough to eat or drink.

"I was mulluckin' back pints and now I'm full as an egg!"

Grig (v.)
To slag someone off.

"Stop griggin' me or i'll bayte the head off ya."

For Focal Sake!

Haggart / Haggard (n.)
Very small plot of land.

"Put the sow in de haggart an' don't let her out 'till she gives back de remote control!"

I'd ate de back door buttered (exp.)
Fairly hungry. Someone who would eat a cow between two bread vans.

Jip (adj.)
Physical pain, can also describe slagging.

"De oul knee is givin me jip tonight!"

Her face will kaype her pure (exp.)
A girl so ugly that when she entered an ugly contest they said 'sorry no professionals.'

"Johnny, yer sisters face will keep her pure!"

Jonnick (n.)
Having fun / crack.

"We had bottles of looney soup in Naynagh and we had great jonnick altogether."

[**see also:** gallery: Kilkenny, crack, buzz etc.]

Looney juice / soup (n.)
Cider (generally inexpensive brands).

"I'm as sick as a small hospital after a feed of looney juice last night, 'tis pure lunatic soup!"

Lower The Blades (n.)

Instruction to get tough in a GAA match.

"Lower de blades biys! Up da Premier!"

Muffin (n.)

A woman's private bit.

"And then she said, 'you can put your candle in my birthday muffin any day sonny Jim!'"

Mickey, acting de (exp.)

Someone who does something annoying.

"Stop actin' de mickey an' gimme de sliothar."

Needle (adv.)

A dispute where there is strong disagreement.

"Lads come on will yee, dere's a bit of a needle goin' on over the sliothar."

Ocky / Jobby (n.)

Childish term for faeces.

"Mimmy, I made an ocky in me cacks."

Pandie (n.)

Creamed mashed potato for babies.

"I must make pandie for de peteen ban."

Pure Solid Finesht (adj.)

The absolute best.

"Dat pandie is de pure solid finesht mammy!"

For Focal Sake!

Sozzled (n.)
Drunk as a skunk.

"Yer sozzled, lay off de looney soop biy!"

Tinx (adv.)
Thanks as pronounced in the Cahir area.

"Tinx for putting de kittle on Mimmy!"

Up the Mayor's hole in Cashel
A sarcastic response to someone requesting the geographic co-ordinates of another.

Mickey: *"Johnny, where's teacher?"*|
Johnny: *"Up de Mayor's hole in Cashel!"*

Wearin' the face off (exp.)
Kissing passionately without reserve.

"Look at me man, wearin the face off her!"
"Say nahin' and keep on sayin' it!"

We put him down well (exp.)
The deceased was given a good send off at the wake / funeral.

"Jay lads, we put him down well last night!"

Whisht (adv.)
Expression to tell someone to desist from speaking and begin to listen with intention.

"Whisht, look at yer wan…"
"I wouldn't touch her with yours Paddy!"

Dublin: Metropolitans

As Gaeilge: Baile Átha Cliath (Town of the Ford of Hurdles)
Province: Leinster
County Town: Dublin
Known as: The Metropolitans
Nickname: The Dubs, Jackeens
Colours: Sky Blue & Navy Blue
Song: Molly Malone
Funny Places: Slutsend, Stillorgan, Ballsbridge, Beggarsbush

Dublin, a.k.a. the big smoke (or schmoke, as said in a culchie accent) is Ireland's most densely populated county. To Dubliners all outsiders are known as culchies or boggers (yes that includes Cork people) and to the rest of the country, Dubliners are known as "de Dubs" or Jackeens. Dublin City is made up of two distinct tribes. You have the Southsiders, who say things like "the Dualler" to describe the motorway, and Northsiders, who say things like "Stowreee buud," which means hello. Even though Co. Dublin is extensively urbanised, it has some beautiful scenery along its coast and in its mountains. It also has many areas where wildlife is protected by law (including the Temple Bar area).

For Focal Sake!

Are ye starting are ye? (exp.)

Literal translation: "Are you instigating man-to-man combat?" It can sometimes be taken as an invitation to combat.

Gurrier: *"Smella benjy off yer moth!"*
Skanger: *"Ye startin' are ye? Go hang yer bollix off de five lamps!!!"*

Acting the maggeh (exp.)

A description of someone involved in horseplay, maggeh being the Dubinese for maggot.

"Gerrouradatgarden and stop acting de maggeh ye bleedin' muppeh!"

Ask me arse (exp.)

An impolite way of saying no to someone whilst instructing them to feck off. "Go and shyte" is often used as an alternative.

"Tell Anto, if he doesn't like me sambos, he can go ask me arse!"

Aw-ree (exp.)

Dublin pronunciation of the word alright, often used as a form of greeting.

Tout: *"Aw-ree bud. Get yer hats, scarves and head bands... owny fiyev yeweroh!"*
Fan: *"Shurrup wudja... yev a mouth like a Malahide cod on ya!"*

Batter Boorger (n.)

A favourite cuisine of the Dubs after a good night out on the gargle.

"Howaya luv, would ye like anyting with yer batter boorger tonight, ye ri-yed?"

Bleedin' (adj.)

One of the most overused words in Dublinese. Bleedin' can be placed in front of any word but is generally used in a negative context e.g.

"Ye bleedin sap / muppeh" = You stupid idiot!
"Ye bleedin rat" = Why you informant you!
"Bleedin woegious" = Unbelievably terrible!

Daniel Day (n.)

Rhyming slang for the Luas Transport system, after the famous two-time Oscar winning actor.

"Ah deadly, I thought we missed de Daniel Day Luas there for a minneh!"

Deadly (adj.)

This infectious term originated in Dublin but has since travelled the length and breadth of the country. Can be followed with several words including buzz, rapid and others.

"Did ye hear Ireland got a new manager?"
"Ah deadly buzz!"

For Focal Sake!

Double Bagger (n.)

Someone so ugly, even the tide wouldn't take them out.

"I had to wear a bag meself girl, in case his fell off!!!"

Eevenin' Heddild (n.)

The Evening Herald newspaper as sold on Westmorland Street in Dublin.

"Eevenin' Heddild… get yer Eevenin' Heddild!"

Flowers, in me (exp.)

Expression used to describe when a female is going through her menstrual cycle.

"Sorry luv, not tonight, I'm in me flowers… de pitch, as they say, is well and truly flooded."

Gargle (n.)

Alcoholic beverages. Can be used to as an alternative to "going out on the town."

"I'm headin' out on de gargle tonight, I'll be gee-eyed and elephants drunk later on!"

Gicker (n.)

The anus / hole, also known as one's hoop. In rhyming slang it is often substituted with Brenda Fricker.

"Meet you??? I will in me Brenda Fricker!"

Massiff, Only (n.)

Something that is great. Can mean gorgeous if referring to an individual.

"You're on'y massiff ye ri-yed ye!"

Meet (n.)

To kiss and perhaps do other stuff too.

Ma: *"Did ye 'meet' yer man last night luv?"*
Yungwan: *"Ah, don't be a dirtbird ma!"*

Moth (n.)

Generally used to refer to a one's girlfriend. Can also used to refer to a young, attractive single woman as opposed to a wagon.

"I'm meetin' me moth later on, ye'll see us wearin' de heads off each udder tonight eh!"

[see also: Lack: Waterford]

Nipper (n.)

A child, generally one's own. Chizzlers is another common term for same.

Bridie: *"Any nippers on de way yet Maggie?"*
Maggie: *"Go ask me arse!"*

Ri-yed (adj.)

An attractive member of the opposite sex.

"Jay Molly, yer man Anto is some ri-yed!"
"Gerrawayourradat, he has a face like a bulldog chewin' on a wasp."

For Focal Sake!

Roiysh (adj.)
A South Dublin, specifically D4 pronunciation of the word right.

"Roiysh, I'm taking the DORT (sic) into town because I'm loike sooo dying for a heiny!"

Swi-yen (n.)
Dublin pronunciation of swine. Meaning someone who is a complete gobshyte.

"Give over acting de maggeh ye swi-yen... yer wreckin me buzz!"

Stowree Buud (exp.)
An expression of greeting where the addressee is expected to give an appropriate response

"Aw-ree... stowree buud."
"Gud gud, wass de crack?"

Wagon (n.)
An cantankerous old woman, generally quite large, packing a serious punch.

"Yer wan is some oul wagon, I asked her could I feed the seagulls and she lifted me out of it!"

Yiz / Yez / Yizzer (n.)
You single and plural.

"Are yiz goin' for a gargle later? We're bringin' de culchies out for de night!"

Kilkenny: The Cats

As Gaeilge: Cill Chainnigh
(Canice's Church)
Province: Leinster
County Town: Kilkenny
Known as: The Marble County
Nickname: The Cats
Colours: Black and Amber
Song: The Rose of Mooncoin
Funny Places: Kilmacow, Mooncoin,
Blackbottom, Killinaspick

Kilkenny is located in the South East and is known as the Marble County because of the black stone quarried and used in its fine buildings. Kilkenny is famous for its hurlers, known as 'The Cats.' The origin of the term comes from a tale involving soldiers that were betting on two unfortunate cats, tied together by the tails and hung over a wire to fight to the death. As gambling was forbidden, when the commanding officers came along without warning, one of the soldiers hastily drew his sword and separated the cats from their tails. When the superiors demanded an explanation the soldiers said that the cats had fought until there was nothing left but the tails. Thus 'Cats' is now synonymous with the word fierce and is where the hurlers get their focal name.

For Focal Sake!

Buh (n.)

A friend or acquaintance, usually of the male variety. Possibly bud with a silent 'd' or a local pronunciation of boy, most often heard in the Callan area. "Huh buh?" means, "How are you?' as does "Huh is she buh?" which can be shortened to "wishy-buh?"

"Huh buh wass de crack wid ye?"

Bayte em out de gate (exp.)

An expression used to instruct the hurling team to beat their opponents by a large score. Unfortunately for others, it usually works, must be black (and amber) magic.

"Bayte dem yella-bellies out de gate lads!!!"

Cats, de (n.)

Name given to the Kilkenny hurlers.

"There once were two cats of Kilkenny,
Each thought there was one cat too many,
So they fought and they hit,
And they scratched and they bit,
'Til instead of two cats there weren't any!"

Like, d'ye know (exp.)

A common term used to fill in unwanted silences in any given sentence.

"I went tew de cat laughs, like, d'ye know, and I had a gallery of a time, d'ye know like."

Mullinavegas (n.)

A village in South Kilkenny famous for its Las Vegas style strip.

"Come on buh, less head down to Mullinavegas fur de night."

Cohmer (n.)

The town of Castlecomer.

"Are ye headin' into cohmer or wha?"

Does be (adj.)

Is / are.

"He does be very fond of de smiddicks boy!"

Flahulach (adj.)

Generous or free with something comes from the Gaelic word flaithúilach.

Situation: A sales man goes into a farm to sell animal feeding equipment and the farmer's dog bites the sales-man on the backside. Upon witnessing the act the farmer says:

"I suppose I'll be takin' three so!"

To which the salesman responds:

"Tanks lad, did anywan ever tell ye dat yer fierce fahulach with yer money!"

For Focal Sake!

Fernint (adj.)

An alternative way of saying "in front of."

"If tha' h'oul bibe was fernint of me, I'd swipe the feckin' head off her with a billhook."

Gallery (adj.)

A brilliant time or a good laugh.

"Ah lads, we had some gallery down de park last night."

Hoult (v.)

To grab a hold of something.

"Grab a hoult of dat hurl now and get out on de field or I'll be choppin' heads off an' there'll be wigs on the green!!!"

Hurl (n. v.)

The real name for a hurley. Only people from non-hurling counties call it anything else. Schtick is also acceptable.

"Let go of me schtick or I'll cut the arse off ye with me hurl!"

Let it in ta feck (exp.).

An instruction to send the ball cross field towards the goal.

"Let it in ta feck would ye, ye mule's tool!"

May (adj.).
Used to suggest definite action.

"You forgot me battered sausage? You may go back to Mullinavegas a get it!!!"

Onion Bag (n.).
The goal net.

"The keeper performed miracles in the onion bag today..."

Strawberry Picker (n.).
A derogatory name for a Wexford person.

Wexican: *"Yer owny a powderpisser!"*
Cat: *"Feck off ye feckin' strawberry picker!"*

Scon (v.).
Scon is an alternative word used in Kilkenny for kissing / shifting / snogging / feeking / meeting / bulling etc.

"Well, did you scon anyone last night?"

Wide as a Ditch (exp.).
An expression used to relay the fact that someone has sent the ball a mile wide. The opposite to this would be, "Straight over the black-spot," which means the posts were bi-sected perfectly by the ball.

"D'eejit was in front of the goal and he still managed to put it as wide as a ditch!"

Offaly: The Faithful

As Gaeilge: Uíbh Fháilí
(Descendants of Fáilghe)
Province: Leinster
County Town: Tullamore
Known as: The Kings County
Nickname: The Faithful, The BIFFOS
Colours: Green, White and Gold
Song: The Offaly Rover, Love's Old
Sweet Song
Funny Places: Birr, Rhode, Crinkill,
Blue Ball

Offaly is an awfully nice county in the centre of Ireland. It has some beautiful scenery, including the Slieve Bloom Mountains, the floodplain of the Shannon and many bogs, including the Bog of Allen. Offaly people are often referred to as BIFFOS, which, according to many, means: Big Ignorant F*ckers From Offaly. However, in actual fact it means Beautiful Intelligent Females From Offaly, which I can personally attest to. Even though only a tiny fraction of Offaly's small population plays hurling, it has had major success in the discipline. Apparently, there is a Rabbi of some importance living in Offaly, as people keep referring to a Tullamore Jew?

Aisy (adv.)

Easy / slow / handy.

"Take ih aisy boy an' have a bag o' Tayho'"

A touch of the stalk (exp.)

Sexual intimacy.

Johnny: *"Mikey did ye give that Sheila wan a touch of the stalk?"*
Mikey: *"I did boy but, she was such a heifer the light-bulb burnt me arse."*

Agin (adv.)

Against.

"The heifer pinned me agin de wall when I told her that even Mr. Muscle wouldn't shift her!"

Ara Shyte (adv.)

An expression of sheer dejection.

"15 yo yos to see Birr play? Ara shyte!"

Back it up (adv.)

An expression asking someone to hang on.

"I'm so hungry I'd ate de balls offa low flyin' duck biys so I'm gonna bail an' get meself an oul bahher sossige okay!"

"Back it up there now an' I'll come withca!"

For Focal Sake!

Brock (adj.)

Broken as said in the BIFFO tongue.

"The feckin' bullocks brock out de field for de turd time dis wayke, jaypors me heart is brock.

Check on the cabbage (exp.)

To visit the urinal for a short spell.

"Lads I'm burstin, so I'm gonna check on de cabbage and strain de spuds alright!"

Breakin de baba heart on me (exp.)

Don't disappoint me or hurt my feelings.

"Paddy, I'm layvin' ya tomorrow…"
"Ah don't be breakin de baba heart on me!"

Dunt (v.)

To shunt or strike something at a slow speed.

"I druv home after a schkinful last night and I hit de shades a dunt. I'm some ngach!"

Fall like a shyte (v.)

To fall in a graceless but comical manner.

"Did you see the ham fall like a shyte!"
"He's no ham, you can cure a ham!"

Hawk (n.)

A nickname for someone from Clara. Not to be confused with quare-hawks or shyte-hawks.

Hurse (n.)

A horse in the language of the faithful. Can be used to refer to a male acquaintance.

"How's it goin' hurse?"
"Ah sher i'nt me blood pressure is up and down like a hoor's knickers!"

Jog / Jag (n.)

A lot of any substance (gabhal in Kerry).

"Get us a jog of turf in de bog luv."

Montaphuck (n.)

Come along now quickly.

"The match is in five, montaphuck will ya!"

Ngach (n.)

A feckin' eejit.

"He's some ngach boy, if he fell into a barrel of diddies he'd come out sucking his thumb!"

Nayre (adj.)

Antonym of ayre.

"Ayre a match? Nah, I've nayre a fag needer!"

Peg (v.)

To throw.

"Put on de kittle and wet de tay there Riha and while yer at it peg a bit of jam on me toasht."

For Focal Sake!

Powerful (adv.)
The greatest possible degree of intensity.

"I'd a powerful pain in me bollix after dat ngach gave me a dunt with his knee!"

Schkinful (n.)
A copious quantity of alcohol.

"I had some schkinful after Offaly won de All Ireland but I still managed to milk a few cows when I got home. I was sick as a small hospital next day though, probably 'cos I woke up under the cow!"

Shaper (n.)
A show off, normally with inferior abilities.

"Look at de shaper with his white boots and, tanned legs in Feb!"

Tellamore (n.)
The county town in an Offaly accent.

"Tellamore is a right spot for de pubs."
"'Tis fair class alright boy."

Up She Flew (exp.)
A joyous outburst, may be heard when the team being supported scores a goal.

"Up she flew biys...
...and the cock flattened her!"

Wexford: Yellow-bellies

As Gaeilge: Loch Garman (Gorman's Lake)
Province: Leinster
County Town: Wexford
Known as: The Model County
Nickname: Yellow-bellies, Strawberries, Wexicans, Slaneysiders
Colours: Purple and Gold
Song: The Purple and Gold, Boolavogue
Funny Places: Horeswood, Bastardstown, Fannystown, Poulpeasty (Worm's Hole)

Wexford is located in the South East and is famous for the 1798 rebellion. The county has miles of golden coast, from Ballymoney to Hook Head lighthouse (the oldest working lighthouse in Europe). It also boasts one of Ireland's finest castles, Johnstown Castle. At some unknown date in the past Wexford took out a trademark on strawberries and as a result it is illegal for any of the other 31 counties to either grow or sell strawberries on the side of the road. So if you see a few quare fellas selling strawberries whilst driving; pull over and support the Wexford economy by purchasing their finest focal export.

Bidda Lord Harry (exp.)

An expression to convey shock or incredulous.

"Oh Bidda Lord Harry, dur quare good rissoles!!!"

Corneh (n.)

An ice cream cone.

"Are ye headin' down d'aarbour for a corneh?"

Desh (n.)

Extremely nice. Most likely comes from the gaelic for nice: deas. Nowadays it has been replaced in many areas by the word deadly, however, it is acceptable to combine the two words together as in "das deadly desh."

"That rissole from Burger Mac's was quare tasty. In fact, it was desh!"

Curse da god (exp.)

To put a hex on something. Normally not meant in earnest but as an expression to convey a Wexford person's annoyance at something, especially in the Bunclody area. In some areas they say "curses o' god" instead.

"Ye et me last strawberry? Ah das quare ill lad! Curse da God on yiz anyways! I'm gonna burn yer house to the axle!"

Dog Rough (exp.)

A person who fell out of the ugly tree and hit every branch on the way down.

"Ahh lad, dah wan I shifted last night dog rough, she had a head like a boiled bollix!!!"

e-Git (n.)

Not an electronic git, but an eejit as pronounced in Wexfordese. Note the strong G.

"Yah didn't do it into the strawberries again did you? Yer some e-Git alright!"

Gicker (n.)

Female reproductive organ. In other parts of the country this can mean the rectum, which sometimes leads to confusion.

"Oh be de lord Harry, I just caught a flicker of dat aul wans gicker as she was togging off! I don't think I'll ever be de same again!"

Girl's Blouse (n.)

Someone who is a bit of a jibber…

"Just ask her for a shift, ye big girl's blouse!"

Hun (n.)

An affectionate term that can be used with complete strangers. Short for honey.

"Want 'em battered or breadcrumbed hun?"

For Focal Sake!

No Bodder (exp.)

Used as an alternative to the phrase: "You're welcome." Means, no problem.

"No bodder, I'll go an' get us a bag a chips, a whurley burger and a couple of rissoles..."

Powderpisser (n.)

What Wexford people call people from Kilkenny, especially in GAA circles.

"Onda model, let's bayte dem powderpissers."

Quare / Quern (adj.)

Used to emphasise a word's importance..

"Das quare ill boy, kicking him in de punnet like dah fer nahin."

Rissoles (n.)

Potato cakes mixed with indigenous herbs and spices, battered or bread-crumbed and deep-fried before serving with a large chip (potato fries). Called a spice burger elsewhere.

"Don't forget ta puh loadsa salt 'n' vinegar on me Rissoles hun!!!"

Shakin' like a shittin' dog (exp.)

A dose of the DTs.

"I was on da razz last night down d'aarbour an' now I'm shakin like a shittin' dog!!!"

Shift (v.)

The act of petting. To physically caress another, can simply mean snogging or kissing.

"Oh be de lord Harry, I caught Johnny shiftin' dah rohhen wan with de hairy legs! I remember shiftin' her wance and she gave me stubble rash!"

[**see also:** stawl, mugg, feek]

The Faaaaait (n.)

Local pronunciation of "The Faythe," a square in South Wexford town. Used as a codeword to spot infiltrators into the area as only locals can pronounce it this way.

"I knew youz blow-ins from Ross weren't from The Faaaaait as soon as ya opened yeer traps!"

We're Taken (n.)

To be embarrassed. Sometimes swept can be used in place of taken.

"I spilt me pint all over me pants, oh lort we're taken!"

Yoh (n.)

A female sheep.

"She's a quern nice yoh for de price lad!"

Galway: **The Tribesmen**

As Gaeilge: Gallimh (Stony River)
Province: Connacht
County Town: Galway
Known as: The Tribal County
Nickname: The Herring Chokers,
Tribesmen, Galwegians
Colours: Maroon & White
Song: Galway Bay
Funny Places: Willyrogue Island, Buffy Foul
Sound, Wormhole

Galway is a large county in the Wesht. It is a very popular tourist destination due to the crack to be had (not the hard drug) in the city and surrounding towns. Galway city is one of the fastest growing cities in Ireland, which is attributed to there being something in the water. Galway slang comes from Shelta, an ancient language used by the travelling community and can still be heard in places such as Tuam. The county is renowned famous for its stony, rugged, hilly territory (or should that be stoned, rugged, territorial hippies on the Wesht shide of the Mississ-hippy?) and, sheep. In fact there are three times as many sheep as people in Galway, so if *ewe* are ever feeling a bit *sheepish*, look focal Wesht!

Beure (n.)
A very attractive or seductive looking woman.

"Howaya sham, any tome beures around, I need a good aul feek tonight!"

Beeg (n.)
To take or carry away feloniously. To steal.

"Stall on boss while I beeg an aul scran!"

Buffer (n.)
Someone that swims in the rural genetic pool.

"Did you hear de way yer man said Wesht, he musht be a buffer from the Wesht Shide!!!"

Crush off (exp.)
To instruct someone to take a look at something.

"Crush off at the cunny feen over yonder... would you feek him?"

Fandan (n.)
Female reproductive organ.

*"Met a sham last night, and my fandan is killin' me all day after the ride he gave me...
...home on the cross bar of his bike ye dirty minded yoke!"*

[**see also:** fanny, gicker, gowl, gee]

For Focal Sake!

Feek (n., v.)

A beautiful girl, called a ride in other counties.
Can also be used as a verb, to feek, which means
to engage in some form of sexual activity, from
kissing to, well, whatever.

*"Jay she's some tome feek, I wouldn't mind
feeking her!"*

Feen (n.)

A yungfella. Often used in a derogatory manner.

*"That feen was gee-eyed after drinkin' too many
bottles o' Bucky (see Armagh)."*

Gomey (n.)

An eejit / dope.

*"His jills is a right gomey, he thought Johnny
Cash was the change ye get from a Condom
machine."*

Jills (n.)

The individual as the object of his own reflective
consciousness. The self. E.g.:

"Her jills is a tome beure."
"His jills et me sammich."

Lush (n.)

To drink or imbibe in small quantities; especially, to take in with the lips in small quantities.

"Giz a lush of yer Bucky quick fast!"

[**see also:** slug]

Lakes (n.)

Someone affected with madness or insanity. Crazy or nuts.

"What de feck is that feek of a beure doing with that feen, she must be lakes in the head!"

Mace (v.)

To forcibly request cash and other valuables from a person under threat of violence (only in Galway could you have two words to describe stealing).

"That sham maced me bottle of Bucky! I'll be wide to the feen next time!"

[**see also:** beag]

Scran (n.)

Food / a feed.

"I stopped off for a bit o' scran and a cup o' scald on the road to Croker!!!"

For Focal Sake!

Skanked (v.)

A verstatile word can be used as an expression of disappointment.

"I was skanked out when I found out I had to work on Paddy's day!!!"

Sham (n.)

A human male. Often associated with Tuam.

"Hey sham, can I have butts on dat fag? I'm hangin' for a few puffs... I haven't had a drag in yonks!"

N.B. One must take care asking for butts on a fag as it may be confused with a request for homosexual intimacy.

Sparch (n.)

The Spanish arch.

"Meself and his jills had a few bottles down the sparch!"

Tome (n.)

Distinguished by qualities which excite admiration; splendid; shining; as, brilliant talents.

"We had a tome night last night in the Gypo."

Wide (v.)

To be knowledgeable about something.

"Are ye wide sham?"

Cavan: The Breffni

As Gaeilge: Cabhán (The Hollow)
Province: Ulster
County Town: Cavan
Known as: The Breffni County
Nickname: The Breffni men,
   Cute Hoors
Colours: Blue & White
Song: Cavan Girl, Ballyjamesduff
Funny Places: Fartan Upper / Lower,
   Killywilly, Legwee

Cavan, or Keeyavan as pronounced by the locals, makes up most of the border between Ulster and Connacht / Leinster. The longest river in the British Isles originates from a small pool in the mountains called the Shannon Pot. Cavan is steeped in Irish history, 6,000 years of it in fact. For example, in a small 5 square mile area, within the plain of Magh Slecht, there are 10 megalithic tombs, 9 standing stones, 8 raths, 7 barrows, 6 crannogs, 5 cute hoors, 4 stone circles, 3 early churches, 2 medieval castles, and a partridge in a pear tree. People in Cavan have been unfairly accused of being mean. Just because they eat their dinner from drawers under the table, in case visitors call around, does not mean they are mean.

Awk shor (exp.)

A expression often used to precede an arbitrary sentence. Most likely a variant of ach.

"Are ya goin' out tonight?"
"Awk shor we'll see hiy!"

Busht (n.)

To physically thrash someone.

"Feck off up the high hole of yer arshe or I'll busht ya!"

Chats (n.)

Juvenile term for the female mammary glands or breasts. Diddies being the general Irish term.

"Look at the fiersche chats on yer wan!"

Chancy (n.)

A woman of ill-repute. Can be used with the word feek as in "Chancy Feek."

"Last night I tipped a chancy feek!!!"

Cute Hoor (exp.)

Someone who is cunning as a fox. Cavan people are often referred to as cute hoors.

"Yan fella's a right cute hoor, if he dropped a Euro it would hit him on the back of the neck on the way down to pick it up!"

Fiersche (adv.)

Very. Used to stress the importance of a word.

"Look at the fiersche arshe on yan fella!"

[**see also:** quare, fair, pure, mighty]

Full as a shuck (exp.)

Inebriated to the point of idiotic / delusional / dangerous behaviour often resulting in headaches, sickness, amnesia, and / or waking up in a cell.

"Awk shor I'm still full as a shuck the day 'cos of de fayde I had last night!"

Note: Shuck (sheugh) means a ditch or drain and can also mean the crevice of one's arse.

Gawm (n.)

An eejit / dopey hoor.

"Ye have to pull down yer monks (Antrim) before ye go for a shyte ye gawm!"

Ohjuss (adj.)

Very large. A mispronunciation of odious. Can also mean amazing as in: "that meal was holy ohjuss!"

"Awk shur, I'm gonna hafta make like hay and bale cos I'm full as a shuck. I've had an ohjuss amount of bulmersh tonight!"

For Focal Sake!

Oh laad! (exp.)

An expression of shock or surprise.

"Oh laad! Yan chancy feek is up the duff and she's sayin' I'm the subla that did it!!!"

Subla (n.)

A scumbag.

"I'll busht ya ye subla!"

The Day (n.)

Today.

"I put an ohjuss amount on thon horse. The day's the day me luck changes."

Tipped (exp.)

To physically romance someone.

"Johnny tipped a bulldog of a wan last night... and she had head like a melted welly to boot!"

Ya Hoor Ya (exp.)

An expression of friendly banter. Can be extended with the word boot as in"

"G'way outa dat ya hoor's boot ya!"

Yan (adj.)

That.

"Yan fella couldn't tell his arse from his elbow so never ask him to give it elbow grease!"

Donegal: Tír Conaill

As Gaeilge: Dún na nGall
(Fort of the Foreigners)
Province: Ulster
County Town: Donegal
Known as: The O'Donnell County
Nickname: The Tír Conaill Men, Herring Gutters
Colours: Green & Gold
Song: Mary From Dungloe, Noreen Bán
Funny Places: Muff, Gay Town

Donegal is situated in the North West and is considered one of Ireland's most scenic counties. Some of its delights include: Malin head, the most Northerly point in Ireland; the Slieve League Cliffs, the second highest in Europe; loughs, such as Lough Derg and Lough Swilly; and Glenveagh National Park, a 140 km² nature reserve with spectacular scenery. Contrary to popular belief, the name for Donegal in Irish, Dún na nGall, is not an instruction for females to close their legs. One might be forgiven for this misconception given the name of Donegal's most infamous focal town: Muff, which before you ask, does actually have a diving club!

For Focal Sake!

Aul Boy / Doll / Pair (n.)

Father, Mother and Parents respectively.

*"Me aul boy and aul doll are always hanlin'
they're a right aul pair hiy!"*

Brute (n.)

A woman of gargantuan proportions (see Baythur
Waterford).

*"I was with a wild brute last night hiy! Needer
John Deere nor Massy could shift her."*

Chutties (n.)

A woman / man's (depending on size) boobs.

*"Staish, look at the bouncing chutties on yer
mawn hiy!"*

Cutties (n.)

Young females, often encountered in Glenties.

Footering! (v.)

To dilly dally around.

*"I was footering around de house all day in me
monks!!"*

G'lack! (exp.)

To wish someone farewell. Pronounced g'luck
down south.

"G'lack hiy!"

Hanlin' (v.)

A heated argument / fight.

"Och, I'm scunnered (see Antrim) with all this hanlin' hiy!!!"

Kooter (n.)

The male / female naughty bit.

"Arra I got a wile clatter in the Kooter!"

Lock (n.)

A small amount.

"Gissa lock of thon ciggies."

Mind (v.)

To remember.

Pat: *"Do ye mind the day it was pishin down and we waited so long you skittered in yer pants?"*

Jerry: *"Whisht, don't be tight hi!"*

Pirties / Purdies (n.)

Colloquial designation for potatoes.

"Pass de pirties 'pon de left hawnd saieede!"

Rare (adj.)

Weird or strange.

"I'm scunnered listening to thot rare loogin!"

For Focal Sake!

Scitter (n.)
A loose motion.

"Arra no, I scittered in me scundies again!"

Staish (adj.)
Wow, would you look at that!

"Staish! The rain is hoppin off the windie still"

Tight (adj.)
Cruel or nasty. Can also mean someone mean as in "as tight as a fish's hole / duck's arse."

"Dat brute is tight with the weeans (kids)!"

Snead (v.)
To kiss or shift or whatever!

"Ara I'd love to snead de head off yer wan!"

Whet de tay (n.)
Put on the kettle for a cup of tea.

"Come on in out of it 'till I whet de tay, tis foundered outsaieede!"

Wile (adj).
Very bad or terrible.

"Look out de windy, 'tis a wile bawd day!"

Yock (n.)
A car or thing.

"Ara, I left me yock in thon yock!"

Carlow: Scallion Eaters

As Gaeilge: Ceatharlach (Many Cattle / Four Lakes)
Province: Leinster
County Town: Carlow
Known as: The Barrow / Dolmen County
Nickname: The Scallion Aters
Colours: Green, Red & Yellow
Song: Follow Me Up To Carlow
Funny Places: Borris, Clonagoose

Carlow, or Carla as pronounced by the locals, is a land locked county, situated in the South East. Carlow Town is situated along the river Barrow and is located half-way between the cities of Waterford and Dublin. Even though Carlow is famous for its colourful parrot-like GAA jersey, it is even more famous for its amazing tourist offerings, from Duckett's Grove (a gothic fairy tale), to Browne's Hill Dolmen with its 100 Tonne capstone, the biggest in Europe so it is! Carlow was the location of Ireland's very first beet factory and even though it was closed in 2005, the people are very up-*beet* about the plans for a bio fuel factory on the site. Monty Carlow is on a *sugar-high* right now!!!

For Focal Sake!

Axe (v.)
Ask as pronounced by Carlovians.

"Are ya goin' Foundry? Will ye go axe yer mudder fair quick lad?"

Blue mouldy for want of (v.)
Badly need or want. Normally used with the word baytin' (beating).

"I was blue mouldy for a pint of stout and when de lad with the big head knocked it over he was blue mouldy for the want of a baytin'"

Biy (v.)
Boy as it is pronounced in Carla'.

"C'mere biys 'till I tell yiz... yer wan is a right buhher-face... her body is lovely, buhher-face is like a bulldog lickin' piss off a nettle!"

Fair (adj.)
Used to stress the importance of the word following it. Very like quare in neighbouring Wexford.

"I do be fair drunk every Friday night in fairness!"

[**see also:** Quaar, Fierce, Pure, Powerful]

Cousint (n.)
Rarely used today. A colloquialism for cousin.

"Me cousint is quare queer lad."

Corb'ya (n.)
To bayte the head off someone.

"Feck off ye poultice (eejit) or I'll corb'ya."

Gift (n.)
General term used to express that things have gone one's way; or sarcastically when they have not.

"Ahh lads, that last goal was a pure gift in all fairness, shocking bad like, me nerves are shot!!!"

Gracey (n.)
Local pronunciation of the word greasy.

"Dem chips were fair gracey lads, lovely after a session in de foundry!"

Rowl (v.)
Local pronunciation of roll meaning to knock someone over with a shoulder or a punch.

"Jaysus dat lad is quare hardy, he'd rowl ya handy I'd say!"

For Focal Sake!

Barra (n.)
The river Barrow as said in a Carla accent.
Sometimes called the Gaza strip as it separates
the Townies from the Graigies (Laois side).

"De barra flows right through Carla Towen!"

The Track (n.)
A scenic walk along side the river barrow, a
favourite with under-age drinkers.

*"Here do ya wanna grab a few flagons an head
down to the track lad?"*

Well Lad (exp.)
An expression of greeting. Well can be used on its
own or with other words such as horse-box, but is
generally followed by lad in Carla.

"Well lad, how's tings?"

Wor (v.)
To strike or wear an implement off someone. Also
used in Kilkenny.

"Head off, or I'll wor me hurl off yer forrid."

Ye Have Yer Shyte! (n.)
When someone is talking rubbish this can be used
to put them in their box.

"Offaly will win the All Ireland this year!"
"Like what like? Will ye have yer shyte!"

Antrim: The Glens

As Gaeilge: Aontroim (Solitary Farm)
Province: Ulster
County Town: Antrim
Known as: The Glens
Nickname: The Saffrons / The Glensmen
Colours: Saffron & White
Song: The Green Glens of Antrim
Funny Places: Springfield, Beardiville, Poobles, Beerhill

Antrim is located in the North East and has many fine attractions including: the Giant's Causway, Carrickfergus Castle, Dunluce Castle and more importantly, the oldest licensed whiskey distillery in the world, Bushmills. The iconic, stainless steel DeLorean car, featured in the film 'Back to the Future,' was produced near Lisburn in the early 80s. Belfast City is the capital city of Norn Ayern and is world famous for the shipyards where the Titanic was built. Belfast was also home to Georgie Best, one of the greatest footballers to ever walk the Earth. Antrim has a strong GAA tradition, especially in the discipline of hurling e.g. Dunloy Cúchullains club, which derives its name from the Ulster demi-god, Setanta / Cúchullain, because of his legendary prowess with his balls and stick.

For Focal Sake!

Ampta / Amtinot (exp.)

A local abbreviation of aren't I? Used by individuals seeking the endorsement of self-praise, pronounced amment elsewhere.

"I'm goin' with yousins for a wee race to the front of the road (shopping area), ampta?"

Away on (exp.)

Feck off!

Brudder: *"Are you seein' ma sister?"*
Friend: *"Away on mate... she's a millie!"*

'Bout ye (exp.)

An expression of greeting.

Mark: *"'Bout ye naaiiieee, mucker?"*
Dominic: *"Ah'm grand kuntyballix!"*

Dead on (exp.)

Great, Perfect.

"The Big Doctor's dead on. He said nothing after I dropped one when he was checking out me Johnny Giles."

Drop One (v.)

To suffer from a bout of flatulence at the expense of one's neighbour.

"Did you drop one? I'm scunnered listening to your awrse, quick open de windy!!!"

Fornenst (v.)

Against.

"Ah brought the bird for a poke an' ah was scundered after she found out ah was on the broo all day drinkin' barrack busters, so she lost the bap held me fornenst the wall and called me a kuntyballix so she did!"

Geg (v.)

A bit of fun, crack.

Millie: *"I hear yousins were throwin' barrack busters down yer necks last night hiy…"*
Spidey: *"Aye it was a geg, so it was!"*

Gutties (n.)

Running shoes. Normally the little black ones that seven year olds wear to P.E.

"Did you see the set of gutties on thon spide?"

[**see also:** Tackies, Rubber-dollies, Buffers]

Knock (n.)

A beautiful female.

"He said he gave some wee knock a poke after she et his piece!!!"

Millie (n.)

A common as muck female.

"Yer one is some millie, Ah saw her shopping 'round the front of the road with her PJs on!"

For Focal Sake!

Monks (n.)

Male undergarments used to protect ones cacks from the dreaded skid-mark.

"Ah forgot to do the paperwork and ended up with skid-marks on me monks!!!"

Piece (n.)

Packed Lunch.

"How many rounds do yoo want in your piece? Will ah put in a wee sammidge or two?"

Poke (n.)

Ice cream. Pokeman means ice-cream-man, and should not be confused with the popular kid's cartoon.

"Do you hear the pokeman? Are ye gettin'?"

Scundered / Scunnered (n.)

Embarassed / Annoyed.

"I saw this millie knock some fella's ballacks in!!! I was scunnered for the poor spide!"

Smicker / Spide (n.)

Common as muck male.

"Check out the geansey on that smicker!"

Wee Buns (n.)

Simple. Easy.

"The exawm was wee buns so 'twas!"

Limerick: Shannonsiders

As Gaeilge: Luimneach (Bare Land)
Province: Munster
County Town: Limerick City
Known as: The Treaty City / County
Nickname: Shannonsiders, Treatyites
Colours: Green & White
Song: Limerick You're a Lady
Funny Places: Effin, Meanus, Oola

Limerick is a county in the South-West with varied landscapes, from the rugged Atlantic shores to the fertile fields of the Golden Vale. Limerick City is an historic settlement through which the River Shannon passes, exiting in the Atlantic, North of the city. Limerick people are renowned for their "stand up and fight" attitude. Limerick people will have a go at anything, and they have had much success in their sporting endeavours over the years to prove it. They have honours in football and hurling, however, if Tipperary is the home of Hurling, then surely Limerick is the home of Irish Rugby. In recent years many Limerick men played on the Heineken cup winning Munster team and in the '80s they beat the All Blacks (which has had a play written about it for focal sake!).

For Focal Sake!

Aboy de kid' (exp.)

An expression of congratulations.

"Ye feeked (see Galway) her? Aboy the kid!"

Batterin' (v.)

An activity performed by little feckers around Halloween.

"I caught the little bollickses out batterin' with eggs again!"

Crack a window open (exp.)

An expression used to instruct someone to open a window quickly.

"Ah lads, who just farted, would ye crack a window open quick!"

Dry as an Arab's Tackie (exp.)

Describes a severe case of oral dehydration. It literally translates to "as dry as an Arab's shoe" An alternative to "Ghandi's flip-flop."

"Lads I was out last night and dis morning me mouth is as dry as an Arab's tackie!!!"

Gowl (n.)

In Limerick, this term means someone who is nasty. One is basically comparing the person to the 'c' word (for vagina).

"Ah g'wan, gimme a Meanie ye greedy gowl!"

Kicked' (adj.)

Someone that is so ugly that you would have to tie a pork chop around their neck in order that the dog might play with them.

"Whaddaya doin' sham, she's not a beore boy, she's kicked!"

C'mere I tell you a question (exp.)

Literally translates to: 'come over here, I want to ask you something,' but it is actually an invitation to hand-to-hand combat.

Mog: *"Hoy cuz, what are you gawkin' at? C'mere I tell you a question!"*
Gowl: *"What are you sayin' eh? You come over here an' I'll kick the heart outta ya!"*

Jizer (n.)

A disco.

"Girlz, are we headin' down to the jizer to check out the Feens?"

Mog (n.)

An eejit.

"I asked the yer man to do bird impression and the mog ate a worm!"

Rapid (adj.)

Brilliant / Marvellous.

"Lads Munster are rapid this year!"

For Focal Sake!

Skittin' (v.)

In an uncontrollable fit of laughing.

"I was skittin' me bollix off when he said Connact were going to bayte Munster!"

Scobe (n.)

An unsavoury character.

"Drive quickly sham... the scobes are out batterin' tonight."

Tackies (n.)

Running shoes. The expression "I took tackie after him," means "I chased him".

"Look at de tackies on yer man, he must be from Stab-a-jax!"

[**see also:** runners, in general Irish section]

Zero Zero L.A. (n.)

American pronunciation of the town Oola.

"Why hello sir, could you please give me directions to Zero Zero L.A.?"

A Limerick Limerick

A Limerick Limerick to finish off this section:

There once was a man from Limerick,
Who spent ages writing a Limerick,
When asked, does it rhyme?
He said, "no it doesn't!"
And that is why he plays rugby!

Longford: O'Farrell County

As Gaeilge: An Longfort (Fortress)
Province: Leinster
County Town: Longford
Known as: The O'Farrell County
Nickname: Slashers (misconception *)
Colours: Blue & Gold
Song: Longford Beggarwoman
Funny Places: Ballinamuck, Killashee

Longford is located in the midlands and is one of Ireland's smallest counties. Though located in Leinster, Longford borders both Ulster and Connacht. Much of its border is naturally formed by the beautiful Lough Ree on the river Shannon. Longford has a long colourful history, from the last battle of the 1798 rebellion taking place at Ballinamuck to the Iron Age oak road stretching over half a mile through the bog at Corlea. Longford has had great success in soccer with Longford Town FC winning the FAI cup two years running in 2003 and 2004. *****Longford** is predominantly a Gaelic football county and has been incorrectly given the nickname of 'The Slashers,' which is the name of a local GAA club. Be very careful if you call them Slashers or they may live up to the focal name!

For Focal Sake!

Bayte (n.)

Generally bayte translates to beat, however in Longford it can mean like.

"Wait an' I tell ya... Biddy gave Mickey a charver... did you ever hear the bayte of it?"

Charver (v.)

A kiss and maybe more.

Bridie: *"Did you get a charver last night?"*
Biddy: *"Are ye lakes, the best lookin' fella there had a face like a melted wheelie bin!!!"*

Jeer (n.)

Someone's posterior.

"Yer wan has some jeer on her lads... I'd run through a mile of barbed wire just to poke a stick in her shyte!"

Jeerwheeze (v.)

To exhale gas from one's anus.

Johnny: *"Ah scab, did you jeerwheeze again?"*
Paddy: *"Better out than an eye!"*

Oul boy / lass (n.)

Mother / Father.

"I wanted to bring de oul boy to the disco last night but de oul lass wasn't having any of it. When he said she had a heart the size of a wren's bollix it was game over!"

101

Scab (adj.)

Something terrible or awful.

"De scraw and stout was pure scab but I was so hungry I'd ate a tinker's toenail and wash it down with the sweat from their sock!"

Skirt (adj.)

Shag off. Can be used in a more generic way e.g. "Are ya skirtin' down for a lush" translates as "are you coming for a pint?"

"I said to yer wan yonder, 'Are ye free tonight or will it cost me?' and without even lookin' at me she just said 'skirt!'"

Wheeze (v.)

To talk with someone, often in a joking or slagging manner. Can be used in conjunction with other words such as "clem" and "choice." E.g. "What's the clem wheeze?" meaning "What's the story?" and "Wheeze choice," meaning, "Keep this information to yourself" or say nothing.

Mickey: *"What's de clem wheeze, how'd de interview go?"*

Mackey: *"Jayz boy, I'm sweatin' like a dyslexic on countdown after it, t'was so scab!"*

Kerry: The Kingdom

As Gaeilge: Ciarraí (the tribe of Ciar)
Province: Munster
County Town: Tralee
Known as: The Kingdom
Nickname: The Kingdom
Colours: Green & Gold
Song: The Rose of Tralee
Funny Places: Ballybunion, Camp, Crow Head, Shot Head, Spa

Kerry is a scenic county located in the South West. Killarney is the main tourist town, which is situated by its tranquil Lakes. Kerry boasts some fabulous scenic routes along its peninsulas, and is home to the tallest mountain in Ireland, Carrauntoohil (3406 ft). Kerry is also famous for Kerry man jokes, which make the local males out to be complete eejits. However, it is Kerry men that are having the last laugh, especially when it comes to Gaelic Football as they have enjoyed unrivalled success in this discipline over the years. Also, only in Kerry could they make a multi-million industry out of a Dolphin named Fungi! The international Rose of Tralee festival is held annually in Co. Kerry, and shows off Ireland's many fine tidy Bridies.

Baguh (adj.)

Used to express indifference to something.

"He's so schtingy every pound's a prisoner with him. He's got crocodile hands, baguh!"

Ball-bag (n.)

One of many words to describe a total eejit in Kerry. Others include bess, dreall, straoll, fastuke, dull amoo, crackawly etc.

Buffers (n.)

Running shoes or trainers.

"I'm in a pucker (undecided) as to what buffers I should get?"

Dayshent Mare (n.)

A fine looking young woman.

"I tapped a Dayshent Mare last night and I got a curgly phian (pins and needles) all over!!!"

Flamin' (n.)

To be drunk beyond one's capacity.

"Do you hear that confounded eejit shouting, he must be flamin' drunk! He's a right who shall he shall (moody), always maith go leor!"

Mopsey (n.)

A naughty or arrogant child, usually a girl.

"Jay, she's a right little mopsy. She told me to feck off when I asked her to wash the ware. She's the devil's painted rip that wan."

For Focal Sake!

Roughest effin' animals (n.)

A designation given to Kerry fans by a previous football manager. This is untrue, however, as everyone knows the roughest animals in Ireland are the Clare Hurlers.

Tappin' (v.)

A word used to describe the act of courting, petting, shifting, getting off with etc. etc. etc.

Jack: *"Jay yer schome beure. Are ye tappin?"*
Bridie: *"Me mudder always said, 'don't run after the boys until they run after you!'"*

Yerra (exp.)

Used at the start of every sentence. As you move northwards "Yerrah" becomes "Erra" until it becomes "Arra" north of Clare.

"Yerra, 'twas hard (cold) today so I brought me flashk of tay with me to get a gabhal of turf from de bog, but I forgot the feckin' ponny (enamel cup) to put it in! Ah pants!"

A Kerryman Joke (or two)

What would the Kerry section be without a couple of cringeworthy Kerryman jokes…

What do they call 'Pop Idol' in Kerry?
Diddly Idol!

Did you hear about the Kerryman who thought he was gay?
He preferred hurling to football!

Meath: The Royals

As Gaeilge:	An Mhí
	(The Middle Province)
Province:	Leinster
County Town:	Navan (Naaaavan)
Known as:	The Royal County
Nickname:	The Royals
Colours:	Green & Gold
Song:	Beautiful Meath
Funny Places:	Nobber, Laytown,
	Trim, Duleek

Meath is situated in the East and is incredibly rich in ancient history. In the Boyne Valley you will find Newgrange, a passage tomb 500 years older than the Pyramids. On the winter solstice, the sun illuminates the passage tomb through an opening above the entrance. Then there's 'The hill of Slane' where Patrick first lit the flame of Christianity in Ireland. Today you will see the flames of thousands of lighters waving in sync as U2 and others sing their ballads in Slane Castle at the foot of the hill. Then there's Tara, the St. Peter's Square of ancient Ireland and so much more. Nobber is probably the funniest town name in Ireland and is derived from the Irish 'An Obair' (or The Work). I would suggest they do a little work on the focal name.

For Focal Sake!

Brownin' (adj.)

A term used to describe an inner feeling of irritation at another persons actions, either physical or verbal.

"Dat wan is brownin' me boy... she keeps takin the praytays without askin'! She's so fat that when she gets a text message people think she's backing up!"

[**see also:** scunnered: Antrim]

Dry Balls (n.)

A person that is socially unexciting. With a person such as this, one would rather commit seppuko (Hari-Kari) than converse with them.

"You'd swear dat chap had a towel permanently wrapped around his bollix, he's such a dry balls!"

Get up dare on yer hind legs (exp.)

An expression used to encourage someone introverted (perhaps a dry balls) to make a holy show of themselves in public.

"Get up dare on yer hind legs Paddy, y'oul dry balls, an' givvus a song!"

Hould yer whisht (exp.)

Used to inform someone, if they do not keep their gob shut you will happily shut it for them.

"Hould yer whisht lads! Paddy is singing!"

How's yer livestock for a bullin'?

An invitation to a member of the opposite sex to engage in sexual intercourse.

"How's yer livestock for a bullin'? Wanna tip to Laytown for a bit of how's yer father?"

Moon

An exclamation of surprise at how peculiar something is. Similar to mental / mad.

"Naaavan won de foball??? Das moon!!!"

Motherless

Intoxicated to such an extent that either one forgets who their mother is or their mother disowns them, perhaps both.

"I was left motherless on the street last night!"

Praytays

A perennial plant of the Solanaceae otherwise known as potatoes. Praytays is an obvious bastardisation of the Gaelic for spuds, prátaí.

"Don't be givin' me de hairy eyeball (evil eye) now Mammy, just get me some of yer praytays, dare claaaass!!!"

Schnear / Sneer (n.)

A replacement for the Irish word crack. Schnear is a versatile word and can be used in many situations e.g "Get up off yer hind leg for the schnear" and "Any schnear?"

Armagh: The Orchard

As Gaeilge: Ard Mhacha
(The Height of Macha)
Province: Ulster
County Town: Armagh
Known as: Orchard / Cathedral County
Nickname: Bandit Country (South only)
Colours: Orange & White
Song: The Boys of the County Armagh
Funny Places: Ballywilly, Ballsmill, Kilmore

Armagh is located in North East Ireland and is bordered by 4 counties and Lough Neagh (Finn McCool's bog). It is known as the Orchard of Ireland because it sends apples to Clonmel to make cider. In exchange, Clonmel sends cider back to Armagh to make drunks. Millions of years ago, some Welsh yungfella called Patrick built a church inside a ringfort on a hill in Armagh. He proclaimed that from this church all the other churches of Ireland would be ruled. In Armagh City today, there are two magnificent Cathedrals, Protestant and Catholic, both named after St. Patrick, and are run by Primates. I suppose if they can pilot shuttles why not direct churches.

Bake (n.)
Mouth / Face / Head.

"Ahhh, hit it him a bat in the bake hiy!"

Bucky (n.)
A popular alcoholic drink in Armagh and other Northern counties.

1. Armagh is situated at one point on Norn Ayern's Bucky triangle, a mysterious area where young men and women frequently vanish without trace, only to turn up days later (usually in a field or graveyard), with no memory whatsoever of what happened or how they got there. The only common link to these events is that the people involved frequently wake up surrounded by empty bottles of Bucky.
2. Ard Mhacha translates as the Height of Mhacha, Mhacha being an ancient Celtic Queen, however, purists argue that it strictly translates as 'The Mount of Mhacha' in reference to a guy she met one night after a party involving copious amounts of Bucky.
3. The less politically correct aficionados frequently call Bucky, "A baddle o' bayte the waieefe / wreck de houshe."
4. You can get a party started anywhere in Armagh, all you need is a crate of the holy wine and "go on de swally," however, too many and Armagh-geddon may ensue.

110

For Focal Sake!

Cat (n.)

Cat means bad, but append melodeon (pronounced malojan) and it means something is absolutely awful.

"Ah hawve a dog at home an' it went cat so it did!"

Conya (n.)

Faecal matter discharged from the body, otherwise known as poo. If an anna-conda is a large South American snake then an anna-conya is a large South Armagh shyte.

"Some garshun was screamin' in the jawx last naight, he must have given birth to an Anna-conya!"

Cowp (v.)

Fall over or push something over.

"'Did you cowp thon cow till its side?"

Feek (v.)

The act of caressing with the lips (or an instance thereof).

"Why cawn I never feek someone munya (see Kildare), ah always end up in the same sitch-ye-ashian evury naieght with some cat malojan aul wan in de Bourne!"

Gahsun / Garshun (n.)

Boy / Fella. Probably derived from the old French word garçon meaning young male servant.

"Gahsun!!! go dyne to thon shop and get me fufteen, naw twenny cases of Bucky naieee bah."

Gesha (n.)

Young girl. Female equivalent of Gasun.

"Look at de gutties (runners) on thon gesha."

Shkin (n.)

A good friend.

"'Bout ye shkin! Are you away to de jab?"

Steek / Skeet (n).

Tracksuit wearing individuals that suffer from "eye-brow-on-lip" syndrome (called a skanger-tash in Dublin). Skeets often wear patterned jumpers (geansies) with tracksuit bottoms and bright white runners to make some sort of statement. Eye contact should be avoided at all costs, because you will invariably examining the dead mouse on their lip, their outward pointing eyes and mono-brow, at which point you will be met with a statement such as: *"Ye lookin' at sometin'? I'll batter yer ballix in!"*

Louth: The Wee County

As Gaeilge: An Lú (Named after the Celtic god of light, Lugh)

Province: Leinster

County Town: Dundalk

Known as: The Wee County

Nickname: The Weers

Colours: Red & White

Song: Longford Beggarwoman

Funny Places: Hackballs Cross, Termonfeckin, Collon

Louth is located on the East Coast and is named after the Celtic sun god, Lugh (pronounced Loo), which is appropriate given that it is nicknamed the Wee county (don't worry it doesn't smell like that). Althouth the smallest county, what Louth lacks in size, it more than makes up for in population, with Dundalk and Drogheda, the two largest urban areas in the Republic of Ireland outside the 5 cities of Dublin, Cork, Limerick, Galway and Waterford. Louth is steeped in Celtic history and was the birth place of legendary hurler, Setanta (Cú Chulain), son of Lugh. Perhaps Lugh would bless Louth with another few warriors of similar prowess and help them bayte the shyte out of their neighbours.

Again (exp.)

A replacement word for the phrase "by the time."

"Again I got home the night was only a pup, so I called me scobies and we got twisted hey!"

Beezum (n.)

A broom of sorts, the kind a witch might ride.

"She did the nut and bet the head off me with the beezum when I got in because I was as full as a bingo bus (drunk)."

Bullin' (exp.)

To have a want for something, usually pints.

"Lads I'm bullin' for a few pints d'ya know, I hear they're cheap as chips tonight…"

Cushty (adj.)

Grand, OK.

"The food in there is cushty once you don't mind getting a dose of de scutters after!!!"

Hey (n.)

Like hiy, this word can be added arbitrarily at the end of a sentence to let the addressee know that you have completed it.

"Jay I'm pure full hey, she'll do the nut when I get in hey!"

For Focal Sake!

Iddin (adv.)

Inside or in.

"He's iddin in the pub, he was as full as a fat man in a bath when I left him!"

[**see also:** adhin, Monaghan]

Scitter Arse (n.)

A disliked person.

"That fella is nothing but an oul scitter arse!"

Throw the head in (exp.)

To aggressively look for a kiss, sometimes without consent.

Mikey: *"I did not throw the head in on yon wan last night?"*
Paddy:*"Ye did ye dirty yoke hey! If I had a bag of mickies I wouldn't give her one!"*

[**see also:** lob the gob, Cork]

Well Boss (exp.)

A form of greeting for one's friends.

"Well boss what's de story?"

Scoby / Zoby (exp.)

A friend.

"Well scoby are yiz headin' over to the far side (either side of the bridge in Drogheda depending on what side your on) for a few scoops?"

Clare: The Banner

As Gaeilge: An Clár (Plain)
Province: Munster
County Town: Ennis
Known as: The Banner County
Nickname: Bannermen
Colours: Saffron & Blue
Song: My Lovely Rose of Clare
Funny Places: Tubber, Bunratty, Inch

Clare is located in the West of Ireland and has a strong tradition of "ceol agus crack" (music and fun), especially in touristy places such as Doolin and Lisdoonvarna. Clare experienced a renaissance period in hurling during the 90s winning not one, but two All Ireland Senior Hurling Championships. Hurlers from other counties are still sore ten years on from the baytins dished out by the Banner men, who are often called muck-savages by their neighbours. The Burren, a unique karst region, contains popular tourist attractions such as the Poulnabrone Dolmen and the impressive Cliffs of Moher. Clare suffers from the E.S.P. phenomenon (Excessive Sign Posts) and it is said that there are more sign posts in Clare than there are sheep in Galway (and that's a lot).

For Focal Sake!

Bagel (n.)

Person from the countryside or of an agricultural persuasion. Most likely comes from a mispronunciation of the beagle breed of dog (given its mongrel heritage).

"Get up the road ye oul bagel!"

Bull, to give the (exp.)

To get a female pregnant.

"G'wan to hell lad, if yer going bovine, ye might as well give her the bull!"

Crusties (n.)

A tree-hugging, stripey-sock wearing, unshaven hippy, with long dreadlocks under a tea cosy, army surplus clothing and multiple nose piercings. Often spotted queuing for dole.

"Ah slur, we'll be here all day with all the crusties around!"

Cake (n.)

Excrement. Comes from a variation of the Gaelic word cach, meaning poo.

"Dat new song from Dustin is pure cake lad!"

Conwraning (n.)

Complaining, giving out.

"Would ye ever stop cribbin' and conwraning, we're goin' out girlin' tonight!"

Gobaloon (n.)

Yet another word for a dope or eejit.

"Did ye hear what that gobaloon said about your mudder lad... flow'r de bagel!"

Has she Feck (exp.)

Expression of surprise. Could be said about a woman with nice breasts or a Massey tractor with suspension.

"The new Massey has back suspension lad!"
"Oh! Has she feck?"

How's yer Balls (exp.)

An expression of greeting with the same meaning as, "How are you keeping?"

"Ah sher I'm grand, how's yer balls?"

Jag (v.)

To shift, court, feek, see etc. someone

"Skutch (scat or geatz) out of it yee dirty feckers... go jag somewhere else!"

Mog (n.)

A woman that is beyond unpleasant to the eye.

"I heard Johnny pulled a mog for himself..."

Slur (exp.)

An expression of disappointment

"Slur, the Clare section is finished!"

Kildare: The Lilywhites

As Gaeilge: Cill Dara
(Church of the Oak)
Province: Leinster
County Town: Naas
Known as: The Shortgrass / Thoroughbred
County
Nickname: The Lilywhites, Flourbags
Colours: White
Song: The Curragh of Kildare
Funny Places: Kilcock, Athy, Leixlip

Kildare is an inland county of Leinster in East Ireland. In the North of the County you will find Leixlip, birthplace of Guinness. Once famed for its fish and chips after a night out on the stout, it is now famous for silicon chips as Intel have a massive facility there. Kildare is also famous for horses and short grass (not the horses that play football in St Conleth's Park, the Lilywhites). It boasts the Curragh and Punchestown race courses, which account for the horse part; and the K club, where the Ryder cup was held in 2006, which accounts for the short grass part. Besides the race courses it is also home to the National Stud (before you ask, Daniel O'Donnell is from Donegal).

Babyshambles (exp.)

An expression used to describe a fiasco or disaster.

"Let's head lads, dis party is some babyshambles we'd be better off whistling up a mouse's hole!"

Cac (v.)

The gaelic for faecal matter excreted by the body in order to eliminate the waste products of metabolism and other non-useful materials.... otherwise known as shyte.

"Á cac! Tá mo guthán marbh."
(A shyte! Me phone is dead.)

Gabhal (n.)

Gaelic for crotch, often used to refer to the female variety. Pronouced gowl by the masses.

"See that feen (see Galway), he's a gabhal."

Liúdramán (n.)

Gaelic for a dim-witted idiot or common as muck eejit. Often shortened to looder. E.g. this might be said about a poor Kildare footballer:

"Dat Liúdramán is as thick as the back of me bollox... he couldn't hit a cow's arse with a banjo... he's about as useful as an arse without a hole!"

For Focal Sake!

Munya (n.)
Something that is excellent or brilliant.

"Mmm... that feen is fierce munya... I wouldn't kick him out of the leaba for ayhin' Tayho!"

Mahawng (adv.)
Exceedingly.

Yungfella: *"I was mahawng drunk last night"*
Yungwan: *I know, sher ye smell like a donkey's oxter!"*

Rulya (adj.)
An adjective to describe someone that is one can short of a six pack or nuts (in a good way).

Frank: *"I said to her, 'I betcha 5 euro I can feel yer Prátaís without touching them' and she said 'yeah right' so I grabbed them and gave her the fiver!!!?"*

Quentin: *"You are wan rulya feen!"*

Benjy (adj.)
A foul aroma that is most unpleasant to the smelling organ.

Gurrier: *"Smella benjy off ye!"*
Boyo: *"G'way ye wannabe D4 gurrier!"*

Wicklow: The Garden

As Gaeilge: Cill Mhantáin
(Church of the toothless one)
Province: Leinster
County Town: Wicklow Town
Known as: The Garden of Ireland
Nickname: The Goat Suckers
Colours: Blue & Yellow
Song: The Meeting of the Waters, Vale of Avoca
Funny Places: Jacks Hole, Hollywood, Doodys Bottoms

Wicklow (pronounced Wickla') is located on the East Coast. It is called, 'The Garden of Ireland' as it is home to spectacular scenery such as the vale of Avoca and Glendalough. Bray, a coastal town, is the largest urban centre with over 30,000 inhabitants and is a great spot for the blue rinse brigade to play the one arm bandits in its many arcades. Nearby, the life story of Christy Brown was filmed in Ardmore Studios, Ireland's only dedicated film studio. If when driving through the Glen of the Downs, you spot something high in the trees, do not be alarmed. It is probably just the abandoned abode of a tree-hugger (crusty) who has since migrated West of the Missis-hippy (Shannon).

For Focal Sake!

Good (n.)

Means "Hello, how are you? I hope you are having a lovely day, I am fine thank you for asking."

Hang fire (exp.)

Wait. Probably a bastardisation of "Hold your Fire" and "Hang on".

"Lads I have to go strain de spuds, will yous hang fire outside?

Flitz, in de (adj.)

To be so drunk that you do not remember your own name.

"He's in the flitz lads... by the looks of it the wheel is spinning but the hamster's dead!'"

Slater (exp.)

Used to bid someone adieu (they may or may not raise you a rabbi).

"Are yous are headin' to town later on? Slater so!"

Shyte-hawk (n.)

A gobshyte, often used to describe someone with a large cranium, metaphorically speaking.

"Look at the head on that big shyte-hawk and the price of cabbage. There's only one head bigger than his and that's Bray head!!!"

Scours (n.)

A bad dose of the trots, otherwise known as diarrhoea, usually leading to a ring of fire.

"Aw man, dat's de worst dose of the scours I've ever had, me hoop is quern sore, and I've just pebble dashed the porcelain throne!"

[see also: scutters]

Targer (n.)

A woman that is impossible to argue with. A targer more often than not gets her way.

"Jay she's some targer, she is like a dog with a bone..."

Wonoh (n.)

Term used to describe a good looking female.

Chris: *"Check out yer wonohs over there... they're ri-yeds aren't they!"*
Alan: *"No bout a doubt it!!!"*

Yous (n.)

The second person singular or plural, used of the person or persons being addressed, in the nominative or objective case.

"I'll see yous later on in Bray so... slater!"

Fermanagh: Ernesiders

As Gaeilge: Fir Manach
(Monach's Men)
Province: Ulster
County Town: Enniskillen
Known as: The McGuire / Erne / Lakeland
County
Nickname: The Ernesiders
Colours: Green & White
Song: Enniskillen, So Many Lakes In
Fermanagh
Funny Places: Gay Island, Noon's Hole

Fermanagh is a landlocked county in the North West, the only county in Norn Ayern that does not touch Lough Neagh. What it lacks in coastline, it more than makes up for with lakes in the form of the two Lough Ernes. Cavers come from all over in order to enter Noon's hole in Boho, renowned as the deepest sumera (abyss or bottomless pit) in Ireland (Reyfad hole nearby is deeper at 540ft). Oscar Wilde attended school in Enniskillen and is quoted as saying: *"Education is an admirable thing, but it is well to remember from time to time that nothing that is worth knowing can be taught..."* Paradoxically, perhaps he learned this tid-bit in Fermanagh?

Ahgoway (exp.)

An expression used in an argument to make light of the issue, literally means, "Ah come on now, be reasonable."

Aul Doll: *"Dawddy, will you givvup lyin' up like a brute?"*
Aul Boy: *"Ahgoway Mawmmy, yer always makin' things a hanlin' hiy! Boys a dear!!!"*

Boys a dear (exp.)

An expression of exasperation.

"Boys a dear, 'twas wide as a ducks arse again, will you put it over the black spot ya hoorsh melt!"

Cub (n.)

A young male, the son of someone.

"D'ye want butther an yer piece (Antrim) cub?"

Cacks (n.)

Pants or more specifically, underpants.

"Ah naiee, the wee scitter did the scitters in his pawnts and it went an the flure hiy!"

Elder (n.)

Another term to describe the male appendage.

"I'm bogged to me elder in this shuck (see Cavan, full as a shuck)!"

For Focal Sake!

Founderin' (adj.)
A state of excessive and uncomfortable cold.

"Turn an the hayte quick, 'tis founderin!"

Give her Dixie (exp.)
To put one's back into something.

"G'wan, put the foot dyne and give her Dixie!"

Hangin' (adv.)
Effect felt the morning after the night before.

"I was loaded last naieeght and naiee I'm hangin hiy!"

Led (n.)
Local pronunciation of the word lad.

Led1: *"Right hiy led, how's she cuttin' hiy?"*
Led2: *"Full of de blade hiy."*

Nogeous (adj.)
This adjective doesn't have a real meaning, when you hear it being used just nod you're head in agreement. Possible variant of ohjuss (see Donegal).

"Thawt was a nogeous sermon Fawder gave!"

Powerful (exp.)
Great / Very. Used in similar circumstances to the words "mighty" or "fierce."

"Yer wan's gat a powerful musclee arse hiy!"

Laois: O'Moore County

As Gaeilge:	Laois (Laeighseach, an Irish Chieftan)
Province:	Leinster
County Town:	Port Laoise
Known as:	The O'Moore County
Nickname:	The County formerly known as Queen's County
Colours:	Blue and White
Song:	Port Laoise
Funny Places:	Borris-in-Ossory, Timahoe, Ballick-moyler

Laois is located in the centre of the country. People from Laois and Offaly are often referred to as BUFFALOs, which means: Big Ugly F*ckers From Around Laois-Offaly. However, the correct meaning is, of course: Bright Unassuming Fellows From Around Laois-Offaly. The Rock of Dunamase is said to be the place where the High King of Ireland's family jewels are guarded by a huge hound. Could this be where the term "The Dog's Bollix" originates from given its proximity to Ballick-moyler? Portlaoise prison, the most secure prison in Europe, is known as a Supermax. However, you still need to go into town to get a meal deal.

For Focal Sake!

At nahin! (exp.)

An expression used to articulate that something could do with a fair amount of improvement.

"Lahs, we're at nahin' unless we bayte de BIFFOs next week!"

Baytins (v.)

An expression used when someone says or does something to offend another.

Paddy: *"D'ye hear tha Dublin fella' over there callin' us BUFFALOs?"*

Biddy: *"Baytins, master wans!!!"*

Be de mortial (exp.)

An expression of sheer incredulity, an alternative to, "Be de holy!"

"Be de mortial lahs, he bet the lard out of yer man for takin' his bag of Tayho!!!"

Briar (n.)

Used to describe someone in a foul humour.

"Yer in a righ' briar today Aniha (Laoisian for Anita)! Are ye not foddered (fed) yet?"

Goo Eyed (exp.)

Loss of bodily functions due to inebriation (gee eyed is a similar term used elsewhere).

"I'm lucky I dihin' end up in Porh-laoise prison last niy, I was so goo-eyed!"

Gocky (n.)

Faeces or shyte as it is known in Ireland.

Teacher: *"Let us discuss the origin of some words. Paddy, where do you think gocky comes from?"*

Paddy: *"Sir, it comes from yer arse!"*

On d'town! (n.)

Guttural war chant shouted at Portlaoise football matches.

"On d'TOOOOWWWWWWNNNNN!"

Tayho (n.)

Any variety of savoury packet snack. Comes from a local pronunciation of the popular brand of Irish potato crisp (chip if yer a yank) called Tayto. If you're from Laois or Offaly, "a packeh of Tayho," could mean Skips, Meanies, Chickatees, Rancheros, Monster / Mighty Munch, Snax, Tayto crisps themselves or any other savoury packet snack for that matter!!!

"I may go lad, I'm mowlin' for a few ice creams (pints of stout) anna Tayho sammich."

Rayle (adj.)

Local pronunciation of the word "real."

"Tis rayle unfair dah rich fella won de lohho... Him winning is like rubbing grease on a fat goose's arse!"

Monaghan: The Farney

As Gaeilge: Muineachán
(Land of the Little Hills)
Province: Ulster
County Town: Monaghan
Known as: The Oriel / Farney / Drumlin
County
Nickname: Farney men, Orielites
Colours: White & Blue
Song: You're a Rascal, Tarry Flynn
Funny Places: Clones, Kilanny

Monaghan is located in the North-East of Ireland. Patrick Kavanagh was born there and wrote some glum poetry about the county, such as 'Stony Grey Soil,' which speaks of the gay child of his passion being taken, due to tough manual labour in the stony fields. Perhaps if he had kept it up he would have had the poise of Apollo like he imagined in the poem. A son of Monaghan, the late Peter Rice, engineered the Sydney Opera House, the Louvre Pyramid and other world class structures. The nickname for the county is 'Farney Men,' which represents only a quarter of the county. Oriel, on the other hand, represents the entire county and so I propose that henceforth Monaghan people be known as the Orielites!

Adhin (adv.)

To be indoors in Monaghanese.

"Horshebox is adhin in the houshe with thon young gesha, d'ya reckon thur bodyaytin'?"
"Aye I'd say they're goin' at it like a barn door on a windy naieeght!"

Bodyaytin' (adv.)

To be engaged in some sexual activity, similarly to bullin', horsin', ridin' etc.

Biddy: *"Did you bodyayte yer mawn lasht naieeght awfter hiy???"*
Maggie: *"Ye have yer shyte! He tried to give me the bullocks jump but instead I gave him the ballix lump!"*

Clatty (n.)

Messy/Dirty.

"Garshun (see Armagh), take the rough off (clean) that horshe-bockshe, 'tis clatty!"
"But Dawddy, I thought you said I haven't the hands to clean me own arshe?"

Halyan (n.)

A rough woman, known as wagon elsewhere. In some parts of the north it can be used to call someone a half-shit eejit.

"Yer wan is some halyan hiy... Even if she hawd two pedals and a sawddle I wouldn't get up on her!"

Horsebox (n.)

Horsebox is often used to refer to a male in one's immediate company. Used in conjunction with "well" it becomes a friendly greeting used extensively in Monaghan. Variants include "How's yer horshe bockshe?"

"Well horshe-bockshe, any crack hiy?"
"Och, I'm just reddin' (clearing) out dis clatty shuck... mon, grab a shovel garshun!"

That's Tarra / Tearradh (exp.)

Terrible according to Monahonians.

"He called you a Halyan? That's a holy Tarra hiy!"

Our Boy / Doll (n.)

As with many counties up north, oul boy / doll is used to describe one's father / mother. "Our boy / doll" on the other hand refers to one's brother / sister.

"I tolt de oul boy that our boy gat arrested for hanlin' (see Donegal) again and he cowped off his chair an' bruk his awrshe!"

Polatic (adj.)

Yet another adverb stress how inebriated one gets after too much alchohol.

"Glack lads, I'm gan (going) home naiiee, I'm polatic after thon fayde (feed) of schtout."

Leitrim: The Ridge

As Gaeilge:	Liath Druim (Grey Ridge)
Province:	Connacht
County Town:	Carrick-on-Shannon
Known as:	The Wild Rose County
Nickname:	The Ridge County
Colours:	Gold & Green
Song:	Lovely Leitrim
Funny Places:	Pullanass

Leitrim is located in the North West of Ireland and has the shortest coastline of any county (about 2.5 miles of coast nestled between Sligo and Donegal). It has the smallest population of any county, the smallest county town and the smallest Christian Church in Europe. What Leitrim lacks in size, however, it makes up for with quality, with 250 beautiful lakes, the spectacular Glencar waterfall and beautiful countryside dotted with drumlins. Leitrim is unusual in that you cannot drive from the North to the South without leaving the county on account of Lough Allen, the buckle of Leitrim's hourglass figure. Leitrim people's staple diet is the original Boxty, which is said locally to "Clayne out even the biggesht of bayshtes," if ye ate too focal much of it!!!

For Focal Sake!

Bockshty (n.)

The home of the rayle (sic) boxty according to
Leitrim people (though Cavan and Fermanagh
people would disagree). Making boxty is a fine
art and if carefully made over a long period it will
clean one's digestive system out. Boxty is a type
of potato cake made from mashed and grated
potatoes mixed with flour. The cakes are boiled
and then sliced and fried in butter.

*"Give the giblet schome bockshty, she's not had a
good oul shyte for hershelf in days!"*

Calf (n.)

A dog so large you could saddle it for a small
adult.

*"The calf is some bayshte of a dag, if this yoke
had come at the young buck Setanta there'd be no
legend of Cuchulainn!"*

Giblet (n.)

Young child.

"The young giblets think Bockshty is savage!"

Horsche-bockshe (n.)

More than just a bit of an eejit, someone that is
completely thick.

*"Me land is more lake than land but I convinced
yaun horsche-bockshe to pay for it by the gallon!
I'm some schkab aren't I?"*

How are you now? (exp.)

An expression used to greet someone

Buck: *"How are ye now?"*
Mote: *"Not to bad at all now, how are ye fixsched yerschelf?"*
Buck: *"Grand, that'll do (i.e. goodbye)!"*

Mote (n.)

One's female companion. Perhaps a variant of the Dublin term moth.

"Yer new mote's is so big she could kick schtayrt a combine harveshter?"
"I don't care boy, ballshe an all I'd give her!"

No Commint (n.)

When a Leitrim person is asked something of a sensitive nature you will get this response.

Garda: *"Can you elaborate on the situation?"*
Local: *"No commint."*

Woll (exp.)

A variant of well.

"Woll, how's she cutting bah, are ye headin' to Drumshanbo to see the lawds jammin'?"

Yaun (adv.)

A colloquialism for the word that.

"Anywan want yaun last bit of Bockshty?"

Westmeath: Lake County

As Gaeilge: An Iarmhí (Left of centre)
Province: Leinster
County Town: Mullingar
Known as: The Lake County
Nickname: The Goat Capital
Colours: Maroon & White
Song: Westmeath Bachelor
Funny Places: Pass if you can, Faggot Hill, Crazy Corner, Crookedwood

Westmeath is located in the centre of the country. Mullingar is the biggest town with Athlone (Arselone) straddling the river Shannon with its left cheek in Roscommon and its right one in Westmeath. At the Hill of Uisneach, the ancient centre of Ireland, the pagan Celtic Druids celebrated Samhain, the origins of Halloween. Another ancient legend 'The Children of Lir' talks of children who were turned into swans by their evil stepmother. They were banished by her to sing at the Lough Derravaragh for 300 years. Westmeath is famous for Ireland's answer to Tom Jones, the late Joe Dolan, who was loved throughout Ireland. Mullingar is renowned for goats and heifers (and by that I don't mean the native yungwans and yungfellas).

Beef to the heel like a Mullingar heifer (exp.)

Refers to a girl with a bit of meat (mayte) on her bones. In today's world she would be said to have cankles (i.e. can't tell where her calf muscles end and her ankles begin).

"Now das the kind of yungwan I'm into, look at her biys, she's beef to the heel like a Mullingar heifer!"

Bayste of a yoke (exp.)

The male version of a Mullingar Heifer. Someone that is built like a brick shit-house.

"Dat fella I was marking was one big bayste of a yoke… he was so big that during the match he struck oil with his cogs and when he stood on the weighing scales after the match, it read 'to be continued…'"

Ell (n.)

Greeting. shortened version of Well. Often followed with boy (pronounced biy) or girl.

"Ell girl, hows it going?"

How's she cuttin' (exp.)

A general Irish greeting believed to originate in the midlands.

"How's she cutting?"
"Like a serial killer!"

For Focal Sake!

Layve it so (exp.)

This phrase is equivalent to the well known phrase, "Forget about it," and is often said in a sulky tone of voice.

"I'll help you tomorrow night OK?"
"Ah layve it so!"

Sizeen (exp.)

Used to describe something of a miniscule nature.

"Me missus said, 'look at de sizeen of dat,' and like a midget at a urinal I knew I was in trouble!'"

Some class of an eejit (exp.)

Even more stupider (sic) than an eejit.

"Jay you're some class of an eejit alright, yer about as useful as an ashtray on a motorbike!"

Thick as a ditch (exp.)

Someone that is solid bone from the neck up.

"Yer man is as thick as a ditch, he's about as useful as a back pocket on a vest!"

Tip (n.)

A quick outing to somewhere.

"Just going for a tip into town for a few mins, I need to get meself a few tinnies."

Derry: Oak Leafs

As Gaeilge: Doire (Oak Wood)
Province: Ulster
County Town: Derry
Known as: The Oak Leaf / Grove County
Nickname: Oak leafs
Colours: Red & White
Song: Derry Air (Oh Danny Boy), The Town I loved So Well
Funny Places: Sallowilly, Ringrash, Cloghole

Derry (Durrey as pronounced locally) is located on the North coast. The county town also goes by the name Derry according to most Irish people, however, to the British it is known as Londonderry. The French word for backside is Derriere, and is often confused with the song Derry Air, which is certainly not about someone's arse, though it has been made an arse of on several occasions over the years despite it being such a lovely song. Derry, the most complete walled city in Ireland, is called 'The Maiden City' because its walls were never *penetrated* during the siege of Derry in the 17th century. Do all such analogies have to be of a sexual focal nature?

For Focal Sake!

Afeard (adj.)
Scared or afraid, probably a combination of the words scared, feared and afraid sprinkled with a bit of Norn Ayern accent.

"You hawfta understawnd whaiee he's afeard of walking dyne thon road... lawst taieeme an awminal bit him an the welt!!!"

Blurt (adj.)
The female reproductive organ.

"Myommy, she was hawvin' a go of me bike; broke too hawrd, came off the sawddle, and broke 'er blurt off de cross bawr!!!"

Dander / Dawnder (adj.)
A walk.

"Look at the bandy legs an yer mawn goin' for a dander. He must be burstin' for a pump!"

D.L.A (n.)
Derry Living Allowance.

"Och, I'm goin' for me D.L.A, I can't even afford a poke me pockets are so emmpy!"

Face like a busted cabbage (exp.)
Someone that is aesthetically challenged.

"Yer mawn haws a face on him like a busted cabbage, he's monkeyed drunk!"

Sweet to the Beat (exp.)

An expression of delight, meaning brilliant.
Alternatives are "Belter" and "Magic hiy!"

*"Sweet to the beat, I'll meet yousens later an
down baiee wulwufs! Belter! Magic hiy!"*

Slide On (exp.)

Away with you, feck off etc.

*"Make up yer maieend ye big lump, are we goin'
for a few in spoons or the swarf?"*
"Slide an mucker an' shut yer bake hiy!"

[**see also:** ask me arse - Dublin]

Shuck (n.)

Stick.

*"He shook his shuck like he was playin' for the
Oak Leafs!"*

Steamin' / Schteamin' (n.)

Drunk as a skunk.

*"I was steamin' last night and dis marnin' is
worser 'cos de weeans are doin' me head in."*

Quim (n.)

Yet another word for the female private bit.

Welt (n.)

Yet another word for the male wobbly bit.

Down: The Fortress

As Gaeilge: An Dún (Fort)
Province: Ulster
County Town: Downpatrick
Known as: The Mourne County
Nickname: The Mournemen, The Ardsmen,
The Fortress
Colours: Black & Red
Song: Star of the County Down
Funny Places: Bangor, Beardy Rocks,
Sheeptown, Balloonigan

Down (or Dyne as pronounced locally) is situated in North East Ireland and is shaped a bit like an elephant. On the trunk is Burr Point, mainland Ireland's most Easterly point, and despite the name the average temperature there is pretty good. Big Bow Meel Island just off the coast is the most Easterly Island. Bangor, a huge seaside town on the coast was voted the most desirable place to live in Norn Ayern by UTV viewers in '07. A lot has gone down in Down over the years. For example, Benjamin Franklin stayed at Hillsborough and after meeting the English he went back to America and issued the Declaration of Independence. Would you blame him?

Clothes Peg (n.)

A nickname given to a person of the Catholic faith.

Cream Bun (n.)

A nickname given to a person of the Protestant faith.

Easy to draw (exp.)

A very plain individual.

"Yer wan is fiersche easy to draw, she've a face like a baboon's awrshe."

Frankie (n.)

Co. Down term for someone from Belfast with a thick accent.

"'Bout ye mate? Frankly, I don't understawnd them Frankies!!!"

Minter (n.)

Brilliant, outstanding, cracking, beyond good.

"Thot was some minter of a score by the Ardsmen, Up Dyne bah!"

Shuck (Sheugh) (n.)

Ditch or drain. The big shuck can be used to refer to the Irish Sea or the Atlantic Ocean.

"Are ye fram across the big shuck hiy?"

For Focal Sake!

Sook Sook (exp.)

An expression used to call in the heifers in for an oul milkin'.

"Sook Sook, c'mere ye stupid aminals (sic)."

Sword (n.)

Yungfella. Young man, lad or boy.

"'Bout ye sword, how's yer balls?"

Steek (n.)

See Armagh. Used extensively in North Down to replace the word spide (see Antrim). Can refer to a male that overdresses in trendy clothing.

Thick (n.)

Generally used to describe someone who is not the sharpest pencil in the box, but can also be used to describe someone with a short fuse.

"Yer mawn yonder is fiersche thick, he keeps getting thick with me for callin' him a cream bun!"

Up Down (exp.)

A confusing phrase shouted by Down fans at GAA matches, whether supporting the Ardsmen (Hurling) or Mournmen (Football).

"I cawn't wait for de tay n' sammiches come Sunday!!! Up Down Hiy!"

Roscommon: Sheepstealers

As Gaeilge:	Ros Comáin
	(Corman's Wood)
Province:	Connacht
County Town:	Roscommon
Known as:	The Sheep Stealers
Nickname:	The Rossies
Colours:	Primrose & Blue
Song:	Man of Roscommon
Funny Places:	Suckfield, Strokestown, Boyle,
	Knockvicar, Roosky

Roscommon is located in the Wesht and is the only landlocked county in Connacht. Roscommon has some very famous children such as Douglas Hyde, first president of Ireland and co-founder of the Gaelic League (now there's a man who gave a focal). Maureen O'Sullivan was also born there and played Jane opposite Weismuller's Tarzan. According to some folks in Roscommon, Cheetah, the monkey, was played by some hairy footballer from Mayo. Then there's Lady Betty, who we mustn't mention... Roscommon is the county town but Athlone (or Arselone as it is affectionately called as it is a great crack) is the biggest town though a half of it lies in Westmeath. Sean's bar in Athlone is the oldest pub in Ireland.

For Focal Sake!

Arselone (n.)

Affectionate name for the town that straddles Westmeath and Roscommon. It is anything but a hole.

"Lads are we goin' skullin' a few pints tonight down in Arselone. I hear the girleens down there are fine looking yokes!"

Buck (n.)

A young male.

Bridie: *"I was tippin' a young buck last night Maggie who I thought was a fine bit of schtuff but when I met him today had a head like a sandblasted tomato!!!"*
Maggie: *"'Tis true what dey say Bridie, beauty is in the eye of the beer-holder!"*

Fierce (adj.)

Very, for example to describe a sizeable quantity of turf one might say:

"Das a fierce pile of bog!"

Girleen (n.)

A young female. Een is often added to the end of words to affectionately describe people e.g. Ladeen, Maneen, Agra-een. Comes from Gaelic ín which works like ette in English.

"Wisha girleen, go out and get us a fierce pile of turf."

Horrid (adj.)

Extremely. Can be used in positive as well as negative contexts.

"He said I'd suck a sheep's eye through a hedge of nettles!!! Ah das horrid bad!!!"

I'll be away (exp.)

An expression used to bid farewell to you present company.

"C'mere, I'll be away so before her indoors starts packing me things."

Ride (n.)

In most counties this term means an extremely attraction person with a huge amount of sex appeal, however, in Roscommon, along with the general meaning it can also mean a sound person or something that was very enjoyable.

"Well ride, yer man I met after we had dat ride of a burger was some ride!!!"

Schtones (n.)

A person that could also be described as a feckin' eejit.

"Yer man is pure schtones!!! Look at him standing dare trying to blend in when he's about as inconspicuous as a shyte on an iceberg!"

Tyrone: The Red Hands

As Gaeilge: Tír Eoghain
(Land of Eoghan)
Province: Ulster
County Town: Omagh
Known as: O'Neill / Red Hand County
Nickname: The Red Hands
Colours: White & Red
Song: Tyrone Song
Funny Places: Gammy, Balix

Tyrone is a landlocked county in the Norn Ayern and is the largest of the six counties. The Red Hand on the Tyrone (and Ulster) flag symbolises the outcome of a legendary race between Dermot and O'Neill to decide who would become King of Ulster. Whoever touched their hand off Ulster first would be King. O'Neill was lagging behind and because he was a cute little hoor (maybe he was from Cavan) he cut his own hand off and threw the bloody thing so that it would reach Ulster first. Smart guy O'Neill… he knew he wouldn't need his hand as he would always have the royal wipers there to lend one! It is said that a Tyrone woman will never buy a rabbit without a head for fear it's a cat. Whatever the focal that means!

Bloothered (adj.)

Exhausted or worn out, used to describe how a person feels after drinking too much alcohol.

"Och, Ah had a blarge of drink lawst naight and Ah'm still bloothered the-day!"

Buck Scattered (exp.)

To be in a state of extreme intoxication due to over consumption of alcohol. Normally buck-leppin' ensues immediately after one gets buck-scattered. Buck-shee'd is another variant.

"He was buck-leppin' about like as half shyte eejit after he got buck-scattered!"

Clabbered / Claggered (adj.)

To be covered in dirt.

"For the sake of St. Bernadette in the Batmobile, take off yer shoes before yoo come in hiy... yer clabbered to the knee in shyte!!!"

Guern (v.)

To verbally give out / whinge about something.

Jerry: *"Are ye well Pawt hiy?"*

Pat: *Am I well Jorry? How could ah be well with me awrse split in two, a hole in the middle and no sign of it healin'?*

Jerry: *"Put in that gub an' give up de guernin' hiy!"*

For Focal Sake!

Guype (n.)

An eejit or gullible person. Can also mean wandering around aimlessly.

"That guype couldn't manage a pissup in a brewery, he's solid bone from the neck up!"

Pitters/Praties/Purdies/Pirrie (n.)

An edible tuber native to South America; a staple food of Ireland, potatoes.

"Gimme de pitters quick hiy, I'm so hungry I'd ate the scabby leg off a septic leper!"

Pishmires (n.)

Ants, can refer to the flying kind.

"I've got pishmires in me cacks and they're bitin' de bollix off me."

Slip (n.)

A young pig, typically less than 8 weeks old.

"She was a wee slip when we first met… but now, not even a sniper would take her out!!!"

Scunner (n.)

A person that is very easy to dislike. Someone that causes offence with every bout of verbal diarrhoea.

"Hey scunner, would you ever shut yer bake and give your hole a chawnce."

About the Author

D'author of dis book is a yungfella called Cian Foley. He's Waterford born and bread (sic) and as such he enjoys stuffin' his face with blaas and washing dem down with a few layarge bohhels of Clonmel chardonnay of a Friday night. A graduate of Waterford Institute of Technology with a B.Sc. in Applied Computing, Cian has worked in the software industry for 10 years. He has a range of experience from posts such as researcher in WIT's Telecommunications Software Systems Group (TSSG), to software engineer with commercial software companies both locally and nationally. Cian decided to put his professional skills to good use (ahem!) and set up www.slang.ie so that our unique dialects are preserved for years to come (and also for the focal crack of course).

Anyway, enough of d'oul bull shyte. The author would like to tank you for buyin' de book and hopes dat you enjoyed it as much as the layarge bohhels he drank while puttin' it all tewgeddar. He also asks that you consider logging on to www.slang.ie to submit important slang terms you may have thought of whilst reading the book… 'For Focal Sake!'